THE SYMBOLIC ART
OF GOGOL

THE SYMBOLIC ART OF GOGOL

ESSAYS ON HIS SHORT FICTION

by

James B. Woodward

Slavica

For a complete catalog of Slavica books, with prices and ordering information,
write to:

Slavica Publishers, Inc.
P.O. Box 14388
Columbus, Ohio 43214

ISBN: 0-89357-093-1.

This book was set in IBM Press Roman by Randy Bowlus, Department of Slavic
Languages and Literatures, UCLA.

Printed in the United States of America.

CONTENTS

PREFACE

Despite the incalculable number of critical aids to the study of Gogol's works, we still find it remarkably difficult to pronounce judgment on the most fundamental aspects of his art. A hundred and thirty years after his death we are still asking such basic questions as: is he a realist, a romantic, a "romantic realist", or a surrealist? Are his characters alive or, as the critic Rozanov maintained, "figures of wax"?[1] Is any consistent development perceptible in the evolution of his art? Together with many others, these questions are still the subject of heated debate, and despite the contributions of many distinguished critics, satisfying answers remain as elusive as ever.

In the present contribution a still more basic question is asked: do Gogol's works make sense? In putting this question, what we are essentially asking is this: although the works of Gogol are highly complex structures containing an inexhaustible wealth of meaning, is there not at least one level on which, contrary to appearances, they display the harmony or unity of conception that we normally demand of works of art? Is there not some axis, in other words, on which the seemingly illogical becomes logical and the disparate parts cohere? The object of this study is to argue that such an axis does exist and that it takes the form of a recurrent symbolic or allegorical theme — a theme which by no means exhausts the meaning of Gogol's works, but rather constitutes in each individual work the basis on which he constructs his edifice of meaning. It is precisely this theme, it is held, that determines and explains many of the most typical and disconcerting features of his narrative art. By examining, therefore, the manner in which he develops this theme, it is proposed to suggest new answers to some of the major questions posed by his fiction and to offer new interpretations of some of his best known works.

The method adopted of substantiating the major arguments presented in the study takes the form of five interpretative essays. After the short opening chapter, in which the arguments are summarised, five of Gogol's most celebrated and "difficult" stories are examined in detail: "Ivan Fyodorovich Shpon'ka and His Aunt" (*Ivan Fyodorovich Shpon'ka i yego tyotushka*), "Old-World Landowners" (*Starosvetskiye pomeshchiki*), "The Nose" (*Nos*), "The Overcoat" (*Shinel'*) and "The Carriage" (*Kolyaska*). Thus one story is taken from each of his first two volumes — *Evenings on a Farm near Dikan'ka* (*Vechera na khutore bliz Dikan'ki*)[2] and *Mirgorod* — and three from the cycle of "Petersburg tales". This does not mean that his other tales receive no attention; indeed, together with *Dead Souls*, they are frequently referred to, and the study also embraces such wider issues as the relationship, for example, between "Ivan Fyodorovich Shpon'ka and His Aunt" and the other tales of *Evenings* and the relevance of the early Ukrainian stories to the later fiction. But the five selected stories, it is held, are not only among his most outstanding achievements in the shorter narrative genre; they also display all the most characteristic features of his evolving narrative method and pose in an exceptionally acute form the major problems with which his art confronts the reader. The view is taken, therefore, that if the problems raised by these stories can be convincingly resolved, significant light will be cast on his art in general.

All references to Gogol's works in the study are to the fourteen-volume edition published by the Soviet Academy of Sciences[3] (by volume and page number) and are entered in the text. In references to the edition in footnotes the abbreviation *PSS* is used. All translations from the Russian are my own and all dates are in "Old Style".

In conclusion, I would like to thank the editors of *The Modern Language Review* and *Russian Literature* for their permission to use in this book material from my articles published in their journals.

J. B. WOODWARD

Swansea
March 1981

FOOTNOTES TO PREFACE

1. V. V. Rozanov, *Legenda o velikom inkvizitore*, 3rd edn. (St. Petersburg, 1906), p. 261.
2. The title of this volume is abbreviated hereafter to *Evenings*.
3. N. V. Gogol', *Polnoye sobraniye sochineniy* (Moscow, 1937-1952).

I

GOGOL'S SYMBOLISM

The most celebrated stories of Gogol continue to defy the most strenuous and ingenious efforts of critics to produce interpretations which account plausibly for the oddities of their content and structure. They have been studied as social satires; as bizarre syntheses of elements culled from operatic conventions, Ukrainian folksongs, the repertory of the Ukrainian puppet theatre and the literature of German Romanticism; as dramatised confessions by the author of his sexual problems; as scintillating performances by a brilliant actor or impersonator; and as the elaborate grotesques of a moralist reflecting his uncompromising rejection of the world. Yet all these interpretations continue to evoke from the reader the same recurrent questions: "What, then, is the point of this or that detail? Why does Gogol include it? How can it possibly be reconciled with the interpretation that has been suggested? " In short, criticism has yet to convince us that such stories as "Old-World Landowners" and "The Overcoat" are "valid" in the Barthian sense of the term, i.e. that they constitute "coherent systems of signs".[1] Although these tales have been acclaimed as two of the greatest short stories in world literature, we still find them resistant to the demand that we usually make of works of art for a sustained, meaningful interplay between all their constituent elements. Whatever approach is adopted, it invariably occurs that discordant details remain to reinforce our sceptical attitude to the contention of the critic I. D. Yermakov that in the works of Gogol "there is no room for arbitrariness or the incidental".[2]

The suspicion, however, that Yermakov may be right, that there does exist some underlying theme or scheme of ideas in terms of which the apparent discords may be seen to form part of an integrated, coherent structure, is not easily banished. Indeed, it is strengthened by the pronouncements of Gogol himself, for a profound concern with the notion of aesthetic harmony is reflected repeatedly in his statements about art. Not only, for example, does he proclaim to the poet Zhukovsky in a letter of 1848 that art "instils harmony and order into the soul, not confusion and disorder" (XIV, 37), but two years later, in a letter to A. O. Smirnova, he observed: "A verbal work of art is the same as a pictorial work of art; it is the same as a picture. One must first step back and then approach it again; one must examine it continually to check that some harsh feature does not protrude and that the general harmony is not disrupted by some discordant cry . . ."[3] If we accept, therefore, that in the mystifying tales referred to above he was intent on creating "verbal works of art", we must assume that there too the elimination of "discordant cries" was one of his major concerns, that even the most bizarre details and ostensibly digressive passages are subject to certain constraints and constitute inalienable elements of "generally harmonious" structures. And if this argument is pursued further, it can lead ultimately to only one conclusion — that the art of Gogol is fundamentally symbolic, for to assert its "realism" is not only in many cases patently absurd; it is also to impute to his works the arbitrariness and incoherence which are the negation of art.

This conclusion lies at the basis of the present study, in which an attempt is made to decipher Gogol's symbolism with the object of highlighting the "general harmony" of the five selected stories and the constraints and modes of thought which determine their character. The objective has dictated the approach. Neither the "anxieties" and complexes of Gogol the man, to which Yermakov, Driessen and Karlinsky relate the more conspicuous features of his art,[4] nor the coexistence in his tales of elements absorbed from differing literary traditions and styles, in which Vinogradov and Gukovsky perceive one of the major reasons for their alleged unevenness,[5] will receive in the study the attention that they are normally accorded. For quite apart from the fact that these subjects have already been subjected to searching scrutiny, the insights yielded, while often provoking thought about individual elements of his art, generally cast little light on the central problem of how these elements are to be reconciled with the total context of the works in which they appear. It may well be, for example, that Karlinsky is correct in relating the cause of Akaky Akakiyevich's death in "The Overcoat" — allegedly his audacity in desiring "a substitute wife in the form of a feminine-gender overcoat" — to homosexual inclinations on Gogol's part,[6] but we derive little help from this observation when faced with the need to explain why the hero's landlady is wearing only one shoe when he returns after the theft of the coat or why the tailor Petrovich refers to his wife as "the German woman". It is precisely the questions raised by details of this kind that need to be answered before we pass judgment on Gogol the artist, and the only legitimate source of illumination, it is submitted, is the fiction itself, the total context of the details concerned viewed as a coherent, organic structure in which every detail is interlocked with every other in a system of cogent, meaningful relationships. Only when the parts have been assessed in relation to the whole do such secondary sources as information about Gogol the man and the fiction of his contemporaries and predecessors become subjects of genuine interest. In this attempt, therefore, to determine the manner in which the typical Gogolian tale functions as a work of art the search throughout is for all-embracing patterns of meaning which are suggested principally by the coexistence of elements within the same aesthetic context.

At the same time it must be stated at once that a certain modification of this approach is considered not only desirable but essential. In any attempt, it is held, to decipher the meaning of the individual Gogolian tale there is one particular type of extraneous support that must repeatedly be invoked — namely, that provided by his other works. In other words, the exercise of assessing individual elements of a given story in relation to the other elements which comprise their context must frequently be complemented by that of assessing them in relation to the same elements in other Gogolian contexts. Doubtless the eyebrows of the purists will immediately be raised, but the validity of this procedure may be defended by reference to one of the more distinctive features of Gogol's works which might perhaps be related, in part, to the brevity of the period in which they were written — namely, their unusual homogeneity. If we exclude the decade of torment inflicted by the second volume of *Dead Souls*, Gogol's literary career, like that of Lermontov who was similarly given to repeating himself, extended over only thirteen years (1829-1842), ending when he had reached an age (thirty-three) at which Tolstoy, Turgenev and Dostoyevsky had respectively two, six and eleven years to wait before beginning work on their first major novels. Moreover, the periods of composition of individual works frequently overlapped and, as if to stress that the overlaps were not only temporal, Gogol was disposed to arrange them in cycles and even to indicate the existence of links between these larger units. Thus *Mirgorod* originally bore the subtitle "Tales Serving as a Continuation of *Evenings on a Farm near Dikan'ka*". It comes as no surprise, therefore, to find repeatedly in his works variations of the same character-types and plot situations,[7] particular types of relationship and, perhaps most conspicuously, specific groups of details which become almost predictable in certain kinds of context and ultimately give the impression of comprising a common substratum which Gogol had evidently elaborated as a fundamental expressive element of his art from the very beginning. Seemingly inconsequential examples are the repeated references in his works to smoking, pipes, tobacco and snuff, of which, for instance, there are three in his first story "The Sorochintsy Fair" (*Sorochinskaya yarmarka*), six in "Christmas Eve" (*Noch' pered rozhdestvom*), eight in the play *Marriage* (*Zhenit'ba*) and as many as eighteen in the story "Viy", anticipating their recurrence in the portraits of Manilov, Nozdryov and the postmaster in *Dead Souls*. Similarly birds, eggs, flies, dogs, cats, pigs, cucumbers, melons, pumpkins, turnips, guns, swords, drums, sugar, honey, nuts and numerous other details which appear to be equally lacking in intrinsic importance are all liberally sprinkled throughout his *oeuvre*, appearing so frequently and often in such curious contexts that the tendency of critics to group them under such headings as "viscous social landscape painting"[8] soon begins to seem more than a little inadequate. Their persistent intrusions into descriptive passages, dialogues, asides and similes merely reinforce the suspicion that they form part of a single symbolic system that embraces Gogol's fiction in its totality.

Although, therefore, the aesthetic autonomy of each individual tale will repeatedly be affirmed in this study, Gukovsky, it is held, has indicated a cardinal feature of Gogol's art with his statement that his works "present themselves as the parts of a single work of art which are related to one another and cast light on one another".[9] It is precisely this unusually close relationship between his works that justifies the type of comparative approach mentioned above, and the reason for stressing this point is that the need to pass beyond the individual work that is being examined is felt continually due to another feature of his art which is illustrated perhaps most vividly by the postponement till the last chapter of *Dead Souls* of Chichikov's biography and the most explicit disclosure of his fraudulent scheme — namely, Gogol's habit of making extensive use of crucial details and symbols before providing the most revealing hints of their meaning. Far from being confined to individual works, this procedure is repeatedly encountered in his *oeuvre* as a whole viewed as "a single work of art", explaining why it is frequently necessary to turn even to *Dead Souls* itself for clarification of the meaning of details in his three volumes of stories.

Significantly, however, there is one instance in which Gogol conspicuously departs from this practice. In this case he not only leaves us with something more than a collation of fictional contexts on which to base our conclusions but even provides it at the very outset of his literary career. Even before his first collection of stories appeared he published the revealing dialogue between Plato and his disciple Telecles to which he gave the title "Woman" (*Zhenshchina*) (1831). Hitherto critics have usually regarded this curious piece, written in a highly elevated style, as little more than a reflection of Gogol's youthful infatuation with the philosophy of German Idealism and German Romanticism[10] — in particular, with the concept of *das Ewig-Weibliche* — and have tended to deny it any significant claim on our attention.[11] The one exception is Karlinsky, who in his recent study of Gogol's "sexual labyrinth" discusses it at length and rightly claims for it a position of considerable importance in relation to Gogol's subsequent works.[12] To agree with the claim, however, is not necessarily to agree with the argument on which Karlinsky bases it — namely, that "Woman" contains early indications of the homosexual tendencies that he sees continually reflected in the later art. Since the piece consists almost entirely of a lavish paean to the female of the species, it is hardly surprising that even the slender supporting evidence that he does contrive to glean from it is far from conclusive. The importance of the dialogue, it is suggested, lies not in the additional pretext that it provides for probing the recesses of Gogol's psyche, but in the light that it casts on the symbolic system which lies at the basis of his art.

The main source of this light are the following words taken from Plato's eulogy:

> We mature and attain to perfection. But when? When we under-
> stand woman more deeply and completely . . . What is woman? She
> is the language of the gods! We marvel at the gentle, noble coun-
> tenance of a man, but it is not a likeness to the gods that we
> contemplate in him; we perceive the woman in him, we marvel at the
> woman in him, and only in her do we marvel at the gods . . . Why,
> then, does the artist strive with such unappeased desire to transform
> his immortal idea into crude matter and to subject it to our ordinary

senses? Because he is guided by a single sublime emotion — to express the divine in matter itself, to make at least a part of the infinite world of his soul accessible to people, to embody the woman in man (VIII, 145-6).

Employing here the terms "man" and "woman" as metaphors respectively of the human and the divine,[13] of the physical and spiritual aspects of the human personality, Gogol reveals the foundation on which he built his unique metaphorical universe and indirectly explains the self-evident deficiencies of his portraits of female beauty. As symbols of the undefiled human soul, the few untarnished females who inhabit his fictional world were unamenable by their very nature to transmutation into flesh and blood.

Plato's statement that the artist's most sublime aspiration is "to embody the woman in man" not only proclaims at the outset of Gogol's literary career the primarily moral emphasis of his art; it also pre-announces the symbolic forms in which contrasting conditions of the soul were mainly to be represented in his works. While purity of soul was to be conveyed by the idealized feminine attributes with which he later endowed the governor's daughter in *Dead Souls* and Annunziata in "Rome" (*Rim*), conventional masculine attributes — for example, imposing physical size, pugnacity, a propensity to violence and the urge to dominate — were to be his principal means of expressing perversion, commitment to the life of the body.[14] Hence the prominence of certain or all of these latter features not only in the portraits of such males as Chichikov, Nozdryov and Sobakevich (in *Dead Souls*), but also in those of most of his female characters, for example the domineering Agafiya Fedoseyevna ("the lady who bit off the assessor's ear" (II, 223)) in "The Tale of How Ivan Ivanovich Quarrelled with Ivan Nikiforovich" (*Povest' o tom, kak possorilsya Ivan Ivanovich s Ivanom Nikiforovichem*)[15] and (again in *Dead Souls*) the formidable ladies of the town of N. and the equally, if less obviously, dictatorial Korobochka. And it may be noted that although none of these features is apparent in the portrait of the beautiful female who lures Piskaryov in "Nevsky Prospect", her state of corruption is nevertheless signified by the fact that "she has become," in the narrator's words, "a strange, ambiguous creature"; "together with her purity of soul," he adds, "she has lost everything feminine and repulsively appropriated the tricks and insolence of a man, ceasing to be the weak beautiful creature that is so different from us" (III, 21). These portraits show clearly that even though Gogol never succeeded in "embodying the woman in man" and endowed all his male characters with symbolic masculine attributes, the distinction between "masculinity" and "femininity" in his works is essentially unrelated to the sexual distinction. Portraying the overwhelming majority of his female characters as conspicuously more masculine than their male partners or associates, he conveys succinctly, in the form of this contradiction between biological and psychological sexual characteristics, a graphic perversion of the ideal. Indeed, with the exception of the uniquely asexual, "naturalized" Plyushkin in *Dead Souls*,[16] the masculinized female is the embodiment in certain of her guises of the most extreme form of spiritual perversion that we meet in his works. She is one of his earliest and most sustained character-types, testifying less to the misogyny of Gogol the man than to the dilemma of the artist who aspired "to embody the woman in man" and was obliged instead "to embody the man in woman".

The task, however, of "embodying the man in woman" not only gave birth to a recurrent character-type; it also inspired Gogol's most recurrent theme. For the expression of his profoundly pessimistic view of contemporary Russian life he developed an allegorical drama which he placed at the basis of almost all his major works: the drama of the masculine male confronted with the more potent masculinity of the masculinized female and reduced, almost without exception, to a state of pathetic impotence or emasculation. In each case the sexes are placed in a relationship of overt or latent hostility reflecting a struggle for masculine ascendancy in which the female is seldom defeated. It is a theme, therefore, which hinges on a clash between two types of masculine personality or, more precisely, between two clearly defined combinations of masculine psychological characteristics. Personifications of the first type are reckless, combative, profligate individuals, ebullient extroverts with a taste for violence, while the dominant attributes of the second type are tenacity, acquisitiveness, misanthropy and authoritarianism. The contrast between the two types was ultimately to receive perhaps its clearest expression not in the form of a dramatized clash between male and female but in the juxtaposed portraits in *Dead Souls* of Nozdryov and Sobakevich, whose common antipathy to the female is unambiguously conveyed by the fates of their wives (respectively premature death and comprehensive "defeminization"[17]), and the order in which these portraits are presented expresses a point of some importance. The positioning of Sobakevich in the lower circle of Gogol's "Inferno"[18] connotes the greater degree of corruption, and thus the more formidable evil, signified by the attributes that he embodies. Nor is the reasoning difficult to comprehend, for the introverted, suspicious "bear" is clearly a more daunting and sinister figure than the gregarious "hunter" who, for all his destructiveness and addiction to violence, at least displays a healthy vitality and a capacity for passionate feeling. The importance of the point lies in the fact that it is precisely with the more formidable attributes associated with the second, "Sobakevichan" type of masculinity that Gogol endows his masculinized females,[19] while their male partners consistently exhibit, in varying degrees, the "weaker" characteristics of the "Nozdryovian" type. The result is the repeated type of conflict between combative "Nozdryovian" male and authoritarian "Sobakevichan" female in which the triumph of the latter is reflected in the male's emasculation, in the suppression of the "Nozdryovian" vitality which is his most human and appealing attribute. The premature death of Korobochka's husband, her vengeful pursuit of the unsuspecting Chichikov, the somnolence and physical deformities of the males of the town of N., the ineffectuality of their resistance to their wives' demands, the ladies' major contribution to Chichikov's downfall — these are merely a few of the reflections in Gogol's novel of this symbolic conflict that he had developed in his stories. All serve to confirm the observation of the novel's narrator: "There are cases in which a woman, however weak and feeble in character she may be compared with a man, suddenly becomes harder not only than a man, but than anything in the whole world" (VI, 170-1).

The major question, however, concerns the manner in which Gogol uses this theme and the central device of contrasting portraits to create his distinctive, seemingly chaotic fictional world in which everything appears to be subject to some powerful centrifugal force. How are the numerous variations of the theme, which often seem to perform no more than a limited or episodic role, expanded to embrace his tales in their entirety? The question can be answered quite simply. Gogol effects this expansion of the theme by converting every detail of the physical portraits, behaviour and environment of his characters into an expression of the symbolic masculine or feminine attributes which comprise their personalities. Names, mannerisms of speech, the parts of the body and such humdrum phenomena of the physical world as those listed above all function as signals of the psychological characteristics associated with the symbolic sexual identities. In other words, all the basic elements of Gogol's narrative art which so often appear to be capriciously combined — character-portraits, descriptions of setting and landscape, dialogues, narrators' asides — constitute, in reality, super-ficially diverse aggregates of symbolic motifs which coexist in a system of meaningful, if elusive, relationships, and it is precisely in these relationships which cut across the discrete elements of the fiction that the logic of Gogolian art is to be found. It is the logic of a fictional world which is symbolic in two distinct senses — in respect of the ideas that underlie it (the ideas of the "emasculated male" and the "masculinized female") and in respect of the motifs that give expression to these ideas. And appropriately the outstanding character-istic of these motifs, as noted, is their emphatically physical quality. From the most mundane elements of physical reality Gogol constructs an artificial reality with its own unique system of laws and relationships which reflects his vision of a "masculine" world from which the "feminine" soul has been banished.

The sexual implications of the motifs are in some cases entirely overt. Thus one of the more obvious indicators of the masculinity of the two ladies in chapter 9 of *Dead Souls* is their enthusiasm for petticoats which "come to a point in front" (VI, 181), while their adverse comments on Chichikov's nose (VI, 182) seem to allude to the idea of emasculation and may thus be taken to pre-announce their resolve to ensure his downfall. But usually, as Gogol's treatment of the recurrent phallic symbol of the nose testifies, motifs of this kind form merely the point of departure for the development of a whole lattice-work of motifs in which the more or less explicit sexual allusions are soon lost from view. Thus Nozdryov not only sports a name (derived from the noun *nozdrya* ("nostril")) which plainly alludes to the phallic symbol; he is also appropriately associated with creatures with a keen sense of smell, dogs. At the same time the Russian word for "dog" (*sobaka*) is the source of the name of Gogol's other major embodiment of the masculine attributes, Sobakevich. The image of the dog, therefore, may be regarded as a derivative of the image of the nose and likewise becomes a masculine symbol, differing only in the sense that, unlike the image of the nose, it is occasionally used to denote the masculinity of the female as well as that of the male.[20] Here we see a simple example of the manner in which Gogolian imagery is born. Other recurrent masculine symbols derived from the image of the nose have already been indicated – namely, those which relate to the activities of snuff-taking and smoking,[21] and each of these derivative symbols, in its turn, gives birth to its own derivatives. In chapter 4 of *Dead Souls*, for example, the image of powdery snuff inspires the notion of gunpowder, while a pipe becomes the gun with which Nozdryov assaults the "fortress" of Chichikov in the famous Homeric simile towards the end of the chapter (VI, 86-7).[22] Thus from the image of the nose it is but a step to the immensely diversified military imagery which forms such an expressive part of Nozdryov's portrait, and from there it is merely one more step to the related imagery of the competitive games to which he is so passionately addicted – not only cards but also, significantly, draughts, the Russian for which (*shashki*) also means "swords" (VI, 84).[23] The image of the dog is even more productive of derivatives, each of which highlights some additional feature of the typical masculine personality. Since the dogs of Nozdryov, for example, are hunting hounds, they bring in their wake other images of the hunt which, like the imagery of war and games, allude to vitality, competitiveness and pugnacity. And since dogs are hirsute, hirsuteness itself, as Nozdryov's thick hair and jet-black side-whiskers testify (VI, 64), becomes yet another symbol of these quintessential masculine attributes. At the same time the image of the dog in the portrait of Sobakevich seems to express an additional range of meanings, alluding to the canine habit of imposing rigid territorial boundaries and, by extension, to the distinctively "Sobakevichan" masculine attributes of tenacity, authoritarianism, chauvinism and xenophobia.[24] Thus one and the same image derived from the sexual symbol of the nose conveys the entire range of masculine psychological characteristics embodied in the contrasting figures of the "hunter" and the "bear".

These examples illustrate merely a few of the patterns of imagery which are the principal vehicles of meaning in all Gogol's major works, and the connections between them provide a brief glimpse of the kind of logic which underlies in his works the digressive appearance and the seemingly arbitrary juxtapositions of details. Certainly this is not the first study to recognize the presence of sexual allusions in Gogol's works, but its aim is by no means confined to simply reasserting their existence. It is to argue that the theme of sexual conflict lies at the basis of his fiction, that this theme is essentially symbolic or allegorical, and that in terms of it the most distinctive and bewildering features of his art are logically explicable. In the following pages it is not only proposed to show how the indicated patterns of details are repeated, varied and complemented; by examining the five tales in the light of the stated theme it is also hoped to substantiate convincingly the observation of Andrey Belyy that for Gogol the raw material of physical reality is as malleable as dough and in his best works is "baked through to the last detail".[25]

FOOTNOTES TO CHAPTER I

1. Roland Barthes, *Essais Critiques* (Paris, 1964), p. 270.
2. I. D. Yermakov, *Ocherki po analizu tvorchestva N. V. Gogolya* (Moscow-Petrograd, 1923), p. 145.
3. Letter of 23 December 1850 (XIV, 218).
4. See Yermakov, op. cit.; F. C. Driessen, *Gogol as a Short-Story Writer. A Study of His Technique of Composition* (Paris-The Hague, 1965); and Simon Karlinsky, *The Sexual Labyrinth of Nikolai Gogol* (Cambridge, Mass., and London, 1976).
5. See V. V. Vinogradov, *Gogol' i natural'naya shkola* (Leningrad, 1925), p. 42, and G. A. Gukovsky, *Realizm Gogolya* (Moscow-Leningrad, 1959), p. 61.
6. Karlinsky, p. 36.
7. See in this connection, for example, Leon Stilman, "Nevesty, zhenikhi i svakhi", *Vozdushnyye puti*, vol. 4 (New York, 1965), pp. 198-211.
8. Victor Erlich, *Gogol* (New Haven and London, 1969), p. 57.
9. Gukovsky, p. 26.
10. See, for example, V. Gippius, *Gogol'* (Leningrad, 1924), p. 42, and V. Setchkarev, *Gogol. His Life and Works* (London, 1965), p. 122.
11. Thus Mochul'sky dismisses it with the comment: "In 1831 Gogol was still on this side of the fateful boundary; he was a romantic idealist glorifying the divine basis of love and the ennobling influence of beauty" (K. Mochul'sky, *Dukhovnyy put' Gogolya* (Paris, 1934), p. 27.
12. Karlinsky, pp. 26-30.
13. Cf. Gogol's statement in his article "Concerning the Middle Ages" (*O srednikh vekakh*) (1834): "Medieval woman is a divine being" (VIII, 21).
14. Cf. Gogol's indictment of contemporary man in the second of the two letters which comprise his article "Subjects for the Lyric Poet at the Present Time" (*Predmety dlya liricheskogo poeta v nyneshneye vremya*) (1844): "Unwittingly man is clothing himself in flesh; he has already become wholly flesh and is already almost devoid of a soul" (VIII, 280).
15. The title of this story is abbreviated hereafter to "The Two Ivans".
16. See James B. Woodward, *Gogol's "Dead Souls"* (Princeton, 1978), p. 108. This study is referred to hereafter as *GDS*.
17. See ibid., pp. 19 and 34.
18. In reference to Gogol's conception of the portraits of the five landowners as marking the stages of an infernal spiral, see ibid. p. 85.
19. Hence, for example, the many common features between Sobakevich and Korobochka (see ibid., pp. 99-100).
20. See, for example, Chichikov's comparison of Korobochka to a "mongrel" (*dvornyazhka*) (VI, 54).

16

21. See, for example, Major Kovalyov's comparison of his nose to a pipe, in an early redaction of "The Nose", when it is returned to him by the policeman. "That's exactly it," he exclaims, "the very same pipe (*pipochkoy*)" (III, 397).

22. See *GDS*, p. 44. Cf. the comment on the Cossacks' military exploits in *Taras Bul'ba*: "It is only the Cossacks lighting and smoking their pipes" (II, 83).

23. See *GDS*, p. 48.

24. See ibid. p. 8.

25. A. Belyy, *Masterstvo Gogolya* (Moscow, 1934), p. 79.

II

"IVAN FYODOROVICH SHPON'KA AND HIS AUNT" AND GOGOL'S FIRST VOLUME

Regarded unanimously by critics as offering the first major foretaste of the art of the mature Gogol, "Ivan Fyodorovich Shpon'ka and His Aunt",[1] the penultimate tale of *Evenings*, presents perhaps the most explicit development in his fiction of the symbolic theme which hinges on the indicated type of relationship between the sexes. Indeed, the explicitness of the theme may be viewed as one of the more noteworthy reflections of the story's early composition, for in the later tales, as we shall see, it was to be conveyed increasingly by means of the symbolic and allusive procedures which in "Shpon'ka" coexist with more direct forms of representation. If we accept, therefore, the general assumption that the story was written towards the end of 1831, we may perhaps conclude that as in "Woman", which was written in the same year, Gogol was intent in this tale on providing an early explicit statement of the theme to which his art was to be mainly devoted.

Although, however, the theme of the story would appear to be clearly conveyed by the relationship between the two central characters named in the title and has accordingly provoked little debate, three aspects of the work have continued to perplex: the abrupt truncation of the narrative; the curious reason given for it in the Foreword by the fictional narrator of *Evenings*, Rudyy Pan'ko; and, most notably, the apparent incongruity of the story in the context of Gogol's first volume. Thus Victor Erlich, echoing Setchkarev's contention that it "does not fall within the frame of the cycle",[2] describes it as "a shabby comic outsider in the operatic world of *Evenings*",[3] and few readers, one feels, would disagree. In respect of its theme, character-types, setting and style, the story seems to be totally out of place, and various other features of the tale appear to have been expressly designed to accentuate its distinctive character: unlike the other stories of the volume, it is presented by the editor as written rather than told; it has its own distinct narrator; and, as Driessen has observed, "the title does not point to a strange event, a curious place or mysterious time, as do those of the other stories in the collection, but simply mentions two persons".[4] Every effort, therefore, seems to have been made by Gogol to distinguish it from the other tales and thus to prompt an interrogative response.

Before we can attempt, however, to resolve either the questions arising from the story's inclusion in the volume or those which relate to the oddities of its structure, we must first consider the more fundamental question which criticism has thus far left largely unanswered: how does Gogol develop his theme? A clear indication of the theme, as stated, is immediately apparent in the relationship between the two major figures, but a consideration of the manner in which it is developed will not only show it to be rather more complex than appearances would suggest; it will also provide a basis for eliminating the main sources of perplexity and for pronouncing on the tale a more reasoned aesthetic judgment.

Apart from the more modern setting, the feature of the story which perhaps most obviously distinguishes it from the other tales of *Evenings* and at the same time anticipates the technique of the mature writer is the greatly enhanced role that Gogol assigns in it to portraiture. The characters, in other words, are far more clearly individualized. Here for the first time, as the distinctive title suggests, Gogol places character-portraits at the basis of a story, appropriately devoting the two most detailed portraits that he had created thus far to the two character-types which were subsequently to reappear in a multiplicity of guises in almost all his major works. The more compact of the two is the portrait in chapter 3 of the hero's aunt, Vasilisa Kashporovna Tsupchev'ska, which is of such fundamental importance for an understanding of Gogol's later female portraits that quotation in full is entirely justified:

> At this time aunt Vasilisa Kashporovna was about fifty years of age. She had never been married and usually declared that her maiden state was more valuable to her than anything else. However, to the best of my memory, no one had ever asked her to marry him. The reason for this was that all men felt a certain timidity in her presence and totally lacked the spirit to make her a declaration. "Vasilisa Kashporovna is a girl of great character," the suitors would say, and they were quite right, for Vasilisa Kashporovna could make anyone as quiet as a lamb. Without any help at all she could transform the drunken miller, a completely worthless fellow, into a perfect treasure by tugging every day at his forelock with her masculine hand. She was almost as tall as a giant and her corpulence and strength were fully in proportion. It seemed as if nature had made an unpardonable error in condemning her to wear a dark-brown housecoat with small frills on weekdays and a red cashmere shawl on Easter Sunday and on her name-day, for the moustache and jackboots of a dragoon would have suited her better than anything. Her occupations, however, were in complete accord with her appearance: she sailed alone in a boat, rowing more skilfully than any fisherman, shot game, kept a constant watch on the reapers, knew the exact number of melons and water-melons in the melon plantation, took a toll of five copecks from every cart that crossed her dyke, climbed the trees and shook down the pears, beat lazy vassals with her terrible hand, and with the same menacing hand presented a glass of vodka to the deserving. At almost one and the same time she would administer scoldings, dye yarn, speed to the kitchen, make kvass and boil honey jam. She bustled about all day long and managed to get

everything done on time. The result of all this was that Ivan Fyodorovich's small estate, which according to the last census consisted of eighteen serfs, was flourishing in the fullest sense of the word. In addition, she had an excessively warm affection for her nephew and carefully collected copecks for him (I, 293-4).[5]

The epithets applied to the subject's hand — "masculine", "terrible", "menacing" — are perhaps the clearest indications of the portrait's "theme". Not only does it present the most detailed picture that we obtain from Gogol's fiction of the symbolic figure of the masculinized female; it also discloses both the specific psychological characteristics that Gogol was consistently to associate with the masculine type of personality regardless of biological sex and almost all the major symbolic motifs that he was to use henceforth to represent them. Hence the numerous affinities between this awesome female and his principal male embodiments of the masculine attributes, Sobakevich and Nozdryov. Thus the symbolic sexual characteristics of the latter are immediately evoked by the inclusion in the portrait of their two main signals — the "military" and "hunting" motifs — while the statement that she was well suited for a dragoon's moustache reminds us at once of the "hunter's" hirsuteness. Clearly the aunt's closest affinities, however, are with the "canine bear", whose more daunting image is called to mind not only by her powerful physique and by the suggestion that her creation was the work of nature,[6] but equally by the "canine", dictatorial control that she exercises over her nephew's domain, while the graphic representation of this character-trait by reference to the activity of her "terrible masculine hand" plainly foreshadows one of the major allusions to Sobakevich's authoritarian mentality — the term *kulak* ("fist") applied to him by Chichikov (VI, 104, 106-8). Similarly the "constant watch" that she keeps on the reapers anticipates the motif of surveillance which recurs in Sobakevich's portrait.[7] On both estates a single will prevails, transforming human beings into productive automata, punishing indolence with severity and rewarding industry with a glass of vodka (in the case of Vasilisa Kashporovna) or a glowing testimonial (in the case of Sobakevich). Hence the final common feature shared by the two dictators — their aura of imperial grandeur, produced in Sobakevich's portrait by the sprinkling of details which comprise the "imperial motif"[8] and, in the case of Shpon'ka's aunt, by her name, which provides early testimony to the truth of O. N. Smirnova's remark about "the unusual amount of attention that Gogol devoted to the names of his characters".[9] While her surname, derived from the Ukrainian adjective *tsupkiy*, denotes solidity, strength and vigour, her Christian name and patronymic, derived respectively from the Greek *basilissa* ("empress") and the name "Caspar" traditionally given to one of the Three Kings into whom medieval legend transformed the "wise men" who came to Bethlehem, both imply the notion of royalty.

Collation of the portrait, however, with chapter 5 of *Dead Souls* not only reveals obvious parallels; it also highlights the significance of certain details that would appear to be quite irrelevant to the "idea" that lies at the basis of the portrait. It may reasonably be asked, for example: what possible connection can there be between the masculine mentality and the acts of gathering fruit and boiling honey jam? Certainly the answer is difficult to perceive in "Shpon'ka" itself, but it becomes immediately apparent in the light of two metaphorical connections that Gogol forges in *Dead Souls*: namely the association of the symbolic idea of femininity with the recurrent motif of "sweetness" and the representation of violence inflicted on the "feminine" soul by means of verbs expressing the application of heat. Thus in the context of the chapter that is mainly devoted to Sobakevich's portrait the central symbol in the novel of the uncorrupted "feminine" soul, the governor's daughter, is not only referred to by Chichikov as "a sweet morsel" (VI, 93); her portrait also contains obvious allusions to the famous Homeric simile in chapter 1 in which the females at the governor's party are compared to a "gleaming white sugar loaf" that is smashed by the "coarse hands" of an "old housekeeper" (VI, 14).[10] The implication is clearly that such violence is the fate of the "sweet feminine soul" in the masculine realm of the "canine bear", and Gogol reaffirms the point by reincarnating the symbolic figure of the old housekeeper in the person of Sobakevich's cucumber-like masculinized spouse, who serves at dinner, we are told, "neither pears nor plumbs nor any other fruit" but radish jam with hands that reek of cucumber pickle (VI, 92, 100). Here the eradication of the "sweet" soul from the "bear's" domain is conveyed not only by the substitution of vegetables for fruit but also by the subjection of the vegetables to the rigours of pickling and boiling, which on the metaphorical level correspond directly to the housekeeper's "hammering".

The notion of "boiling" (*vareniye*) is suggested at once in the portrait of Vasilisa Kashporovna by the noun "jam" (*varen'ye*), which thus introduces one of the numerous disguises of the motif of heat which is used by Gogol in almost all his works to denote the destruction of the soul by the masculine personality. In *Dead Souls* it appears more commonly in a different disguise — that of the verb "to steam" or "to stew" (*parit'*). Thus Sobakevich, for whom the soul is conceivable only as a vegetable, compares the perverted soul of Chichikov not simply to a turnip, but to a "stewed turnip" (*parenaya repa*) and, in the symbolic guise of the bear Misha, is ascribed with an authoritative knowledge of the manner in which women (i.e. souls) "steam themselves" (*paryatsya*) in the bath (VI, 105). Similarly Chichikov, referring a few pages later to the violence inflicted on him by the masculine Nozdryov, exclaims: "Oh, what a steam-bath he gave me!" (VI, 89), while the *sotnik* in "Viy", the third of the four works in *Mirgorod*, issues the following threat to the hero Khoma Brut: "You don't yet know how skilful my lads are at flogging (literally "steaming" (*parit'*))! . . . Here they first give a flogging (*vyparyat*), then sprinkle with vodka and start all over again!" (II, 213). In general, however, the application of destructive heat to the soul is the special skill that Gogol tends to reserve for his masculinized females, which explains why they are almost invariably cast in the role of dedicated cooks. Devoting his art to the representation of dead souls, he enlists the culinary processes of steaming, stewing, boiling, drying and pickling as expressive metaphors of the antipathy to the soul of his females who have lost their feminine identity. Hence the prominence of these metaphors in the portrait of Shpon'ka's aunt, who not only boils pears and honey but seeks to pickle in vodka the souls of her deserving vassals.

As the portrait, however, of Korobochka in *Dead Souls* most vividly illustrates,[11] the hostility of the masculinized female is not only directed against the "feminine" soul; it is equally provoked, as stated, by the masculinity of the male, in which she instinctively recognizes a challenge and threat to her dominant position. It is consistent, therefore, with the mentality of her type that Vasilisa Kashporovna has avoided marriage and rendered such male vassals as her coachman Omel'ko, whose name, a diminutive of Omelyan (Emilian), is derived from the Greek *aimylios* ("affectionate"), as quiet as lambs. Indeed, given the significance of vegetables in the realms over which Gogol's masculinized females preside, we may perhaps deduce that the unfortunate Omel'ko is one of the "wonderful turnips" in the kitchen garden of which Vasilisa Kashporovna boasts in the postscript to her letter to her nephew (287). And if this assumption is correct, the remark may not only be seen to fit logically into the context of the letter; like the reference to the "dried pears" and "very tasty honey-cakes" that she has sent Shpon'ka since his childhood (287), it may also be regarded as sounding a rather sinister note, as foreshadowing the fate that she has in store for the male who is the legal owner of her domain.

Having determined by reference to the portrait of Nozdryov the specifically masculine implications of the "military motif", we can readily appreciate at least one of the reasons why Vasilisa Kashporovna is so intent in her letter on prevailing on Shpon'ka to retire from the army. Her transparently bogus claim that she "is already old and can no longer see to everything" on the farm (287) merely enhances the force of the symbolism, exposing her request as a cunning subterfuge designed to lure him into the orbit of her own authority before his masculine, military environment has irretrievably transformed his character and placed him beyond her control. She is well aware, of course, at the time of writing that this point has not been reached, that after fifteen years in the service Shpon'ka is still on only the second rung of the officers' ladder. But she is equally aware that if she is to complete the usurpation of her male rival's position and reduce him to the status of another turnip, she must strike without delay. Hence the further display of guile apparent in her reference to his rank as "of no small importance" (287), i.e. as the limit of any normal man's ambition.

Vasilisa Kashporovna's letter, therefore, succinctly conveys her motives, her object and her devious cast of mind. The recipient's response, however, has been known to the reader from the start, for the letter is reproduced in the opening resumé of Shpon'ka's biography which begins with the announcement that four years have passed since his retirement. The crucial implications of the statement explain its position, while the biography that follows explains his compliance. Naturally enough, the biography is usually regarded as a precursor of Chichikov's biography in chapter 11 of *Dead Souls*, for in both cases attention is focused on formative influences which to some extent coincide. It is difficult to see, however, how the argument can be pressed further, for the product of these influences is two radically different types of personality. From their schooldays onward both heroes are confronted with a succession of dominating male representatives of authority, with the "Sobakevichan" type of masculine personality in a variety of guises, and their initial responses are identical: total submission and exemplary conduct. The similarity of response, however, conceals the contrast between the calculating opportunism of Chichikov, for whom the confidence to be gained by such conduct is simply a means of ultimately outwitting his superiors, and Shpon'ka's genuine petrification. Every detail woven into the portrait of the young Shpon'ka highlights the weakness of his masculine instincts. While Nozdryov has a study bedecked with sabres and guns (VI, 74), the "military" equipment of the young Ivan Fyodorovich consists only of a "little knife" (*nozhik*) sheathed in an effeminate "little leather case" which he lends to his classmates only on the condition that they confine themselves to using the blunt edge. Entirely alien to him are the "hunter's" pugnacity, competitiveness and addiction to games which are so vividly displayed by his classmates in their vigorous pastimes, and with the type of forward-pointing allusion that was to recur in his later works Gogol directly relates this timidity of the child to the adult's subsequent experiences. With his refusal to participate in the game of *tesnoy baby* (literally "squeezed woman"), in which, according to the editor's glossary, the occupants of one half of a bench strive to dislodge those of the other, Shpon'ka unwittingly gives notice of his later inability to dislodge the pugnacious female who has seized his estate.

Only once in the career of Shpon'ka the schoolboy does impulse prove stronger than fear, and the result is disaster — a birching by the Latin master, after which, comments the narrator, "the timidity that had always been characteristic of him became even more pronounced" (285). He promptly reverts to the state of mental and physical paralysis which explains why he is almost fifteen when granted admission to the second class. But there he encounters not only more rigorous instruction in the "obligations of man" but also "fractions" (*drobi*) (286) — one of the earliest examples of a typical Gogolian *double entendre*. The superficial context, of course, demands the mathematical meaning, but the noun *drob'* also means "small shot", the kind of shot with which Vasilisa Kashporovna "shot game", and thus allusively reintroduces the "masculine" metaphor of the hunt. With his promotion to the second class, the image seems to imply, Shpon'ka is exposed to increasingly fearsome facets of the masculine mentality. He sees, as the narrator puts it in a phrase that seems designed to reinforce the metaphor with both its imagery and the play on words, "that the further you go into the forest, the thicker the wood (*drov*) becomes" and accordingly devotes the next two years to dreams of escape.

Ironically, however, the realisation of his dreams confronts him with bullets instead of "small shot" and with sabres instead of "little knives": "with the consent of his mother" (his father having died two years before), he enlists in an infantry regiment. How are we to understand this action which seems so totally out of character? The answer is suggested by the laconic references to his parents which provide the most illuminating example that we have encountered thus far of Gogol's remarkable capacity for communicating significant meaning with minimal verbal resources. At first sight these references may well appear to be purely gratuitous pieces of information, but a different conclusion may be reached if they are considered in relation to one particular detail — namely, the hero's surname, which he has taken, of course, from his father. Meaning in Ukrainian "dowel", the name Shpon'ka defines the position of both father and son as that of obedient tools and thus identifies the prematurely deceased Shpon'ka senior as the direct precursor of Korobochka's husband in *Dead Souls* who is obliged by his spouse to perform similarly as a tool, slaving interminably in the muddy fields before likewise succumbing to a premature death.[12] In both cases death may be taken here to denote the male's complete submission to the authority of an implacable female. The name and death, therefore, of Shpon'ka's father may be seen as comprising an oblique exposé of the character of his mother, as indirectly attributing her with the same masculine urge to dominate that characterises his aunt. Accordingly it comes as no surprise to learn that she is Vasilisa Kashporovna's sister, and it is precisely this common urge of the two sisters and the relationship between them that results from it that most plausibly explains Shpon'ka's enlistment in the army. Vasilisa Kashporovna's vindictive disclosure to the hero that during his father's absences (in the fields?) his mother was given to entertaining "a certain Stepan Kuz'mich" (295) not only adds a final touch to the picture of his father's domestic plight; it also confirms the relationship of mutual hostility between the sisters produced by the craving for power that is the most salient characteristic of the Gogolian masculinized female. Having once visited the estate in Shpon'ka's infancy, Vasilisa Kashporovna, we may deduce, had clearly betrayed her resolve to assume control, but in the person of her sister she had met her match — a female of equally potent "canine" tenacity bent on defending her realm not only to the death but even beyond. Hence Vasilisa Kashporovna's subsequent exclusion from the estate and the decision of Shpon'ka's mother to commit him to the "masculinizing" influence of the military life. The statement that Shpon'ka joined the army "with the consent of his mother" leaves unclear which of them first conceived the idea, but the issue at stake in the dispute between the sisters plainly resolves this uncertainty. To ensure the continuing exclusion of Vasilisa

Kashporovna after her passing, the female who has emasculated her husband must now rely ironically on the heir to the effects of her actions. The reversal of these effects is her only hope, and to achieve it, she looks logically to the army, to an infantry regiment which in respect of its boisterous customs, we read, "was in no way inferior to certain cavalry regiments" (286).

Her hope, however, is predictably forlorn. As a young officer Shpon'ka duly exhibits all the symptoms of his earlier paralysis — the same mechanical execution of his duties, the same aversion to his colleagues' masculine activities, the same long delayed progression to the second rung of the ladder. The nearest that he comes to a display of masculine pugnacity is the setting of mouse-traps in the corners of his room. When death finally intervenes, therefore, to dislodge his mother, there is nothing to withstand her jubilant sister's advance. Assuming control "out of the goodness of her heart", Vasilisa Kashporovna can proceed at once to wield the weapon of her "terrible hand", to secure her grip in the absence of the heir before luring him back into her tightly spun web.[13] And from his replay to her beguiling letter she can safely deduce that she has nothing to fear. Addressing her as *milostivaya gosudarynya*, the conventional meaning of which ("dear madam") masks its primary meaning "gracious sovereign", he not only accedes to her request that he retire, but by his punctilious execution of her agricultural "commission" (288) presents abundant proof that he is still a tool.

Looking back, therefore, over the opening chapter, we can see that in addition to introducing the story of Shpon'ka and his aunt, it also provides a fitting introduction to the most distinctive features of Gogol's narrative art. As vividly as the "portrait chapters" of *Dead Souls* it illustrates the crucial importance in his works of seemingly inconsequential details as vehicles of meaning and the characteristic tension of his art between digressive facade and taut, coherent "sub-text". Even the short concluding paragraph of the chapter displays the same two features. Unwittingly condemning himself in perpetuity to the fate signified by his name, Shpon'ka sets out on his homeward journey, we read, "at the very time when the whole earth had turned a vivid shade of fresh green, and when the fields were filled with the fragrance of spring" (288). Once more the irony needs little comment: the journey that will lead to the final extinction of his masculine spirit is projected against the backdrop of nature's renascent vitality. And in the person of his Jewish driver, whose strict observance of the Sabbath seems to express the same sense of insecurity as Shpon'ka's preoccupation with divining his fortune,[14] we encounter not only additional evidence of his immunity to the influence of his military colleagues, who "were just as good as the hussars," we are told, "at dragging Jews about by their curls" (286), but also, perhaps, a symbol or caricature of his own oppressed, subservient status. Not for nothing, we may assume, is their arrival at the estate signalled by an assault on the Jew's legs by one of Vasilisa Kashporovna's dogs (291).

With this attack on the hero's caricature by an extension of his aunt's "canine" personality his fortune is clearly foretold.

The dog's assault marks the introduction of the "canine motif" as an explicit element of Vasilisa Kashporovna's masculine portrait, providing yet another indication of her psychological kinship with the "mongrel" Korobochka. Indeed, the canine welcome of the two males directly foreshadows the greeting of Chichikov and Selifan at the beginning of chapter 3 of *Dead Souls* by Koroboch-ka's canine choir (VI, 44). We read:

> He (Shpon'ka) had scarcely entered the yard when dogs of all kinds — brown, black, grey and spotted — ran up from every side. Some dashed barking under the horses' feet; others ran behind observing that the axle was greased with lard. One, standing near the kitchen and covering a bone with its foot, was barking at the top of its voice; and another was barking in the distance, running to and fro, wagging its tail and seeming to say: "Look, you Christians, what a fine young fellow I am!" (292).

As significant here as the details, for example that of the hound protecting its bone which reminds us of Korobochka's canine reluctance to release the bones of her dead serfs, are the grammatically incorrect masculine forms of the pronominal adjectives "one" and "another" (*odin* and *drugoy*) referring to the last two female dogs (*sobaki*) in the sequence. Such were the forms that Gogol gave them in the two earliest editions of the tale (of 1832 and 1836), and modern editors have rightly reproduced them. Only the editor of the edition of his works which came out in 1842, N. Ya. Prokopovich, felt entitled to replace them with feminine forms (*odna* and *drugaya*), evidently regarding them as reflecting the young Ukrainian's imperfect command of the Russian language. By thus eliminating the grammatically evoked masculinity of the female dogs he destroyed the allusion to the masculinity of the female whom they symbolise.

In addition, however, to the grammatical "mistake" there is also, perhaps, another allusion in the description of the dogs to their mistress — namely, the neatly compartmentalized, "boxy" character of the syntax ("Some . . .; others . . . . One . . .; and another . . ."), which anticipates the kind of rigidly ordered syntactic structure that is not only likewise used in the description of Koroboch-ka's canine choristers (VI, 44), but forms one of the most recurrent and distinctive features of the style of the chapter that is mainly devoted to her portrait.[15] Clearly alluding in that context, like Korobochka's name (which means "box"), to her masculine, authoritarian mentality, to the order that prevails in her disciplined, box-like domain, it may reasonably be attributed with the same expressive function in the portrait of her female precursor. And in both cases the essential feature of the order imposed is its destructive effect on the male of the species. Only one living male inhabitant of Korobochka's estate is mentioned in chapter 3 of *Dead Souls* — the peasant who appears in the gateway shortly before Chichikov's departure (VI, 58) — while twenty of her male dependents are referred to as dead (her husband, her blacksmith and eighteen serfs). Likewise, if we exclude the reapers, whose entire existence, it seems, is spent in the fields (294), only one male, Omel'ko, appears to have survived the regime of Vasilisa Kashporovna, and even he, to judge from his name, has been shorn of every masculine attribute. All the human members of Shpon'ka's welcoming party, like the dogs, are conspicuously female, and prominent among them is the figure of the cook, in whom we may recognize another allusion incarnate to the mistress's plans for the gullible master. And when the aunt who had written to him "about her decrepitude and infirmity" finally appears in person, she "almost lifted him," we are told, "in her arms" (293), thereby pre-announcing his imminent reduction to the status of child.

Referring to him explicitly as "a child" (294), Vasilisa Kashporovna, we read, "forbade him to meddle yet in all branches of the management". Instead, she promptly dispatches him to the fields where, predictably relishing the opportunity to indulge his "toolish" instincts, he even contrives by his efforts to win her praise. But it soon becomes apparent that her praise is no less a mask of her drive for power than her plea for his return, that her purpose, in fact, is to prepare the "tool" for the execution of a more useful task which casts additional light on her reasons for summoning him home. Having assured herself that her authority is unchallenged, she now aspires to extend it, indirectly providing by her method and objective not only a further indication of her affinity with her departed sister, but also an explanation of the latter's extra-marital relationship. As the property of a male, Grigory Grigor'yevich Storchenko, the neighbouring estate Khortyshche naturally represents for her a means of achieving her goal. When it is disclosed, therefore, that Khortyshche's previous owner was Stepan Kuz'mich, Storchenko's uncle and the regular visitor of Shpon'ka's mother, the reason for the latter's devotion to the task of entertaining him is not difficult to infer. In both cases, it seems, the conquest of one male's domain (first Shpon'ka senior's, then Shpon'ka junior's) is merely the stepping-stone to the conquest of another's, and for Vasilisa Kashporovna a *casus belli* already exists — the disappearance of the deed of gift giving Shpon'ka title to part of Khortyshche that his mother secured for him by her potent charms.

The circumstances of the deed's disappearance are left shrouded in mystery. Perhaps we are meant to deduce that on the verge of the grave Shpon'ka's mother, realising the vanity of the hopes that she had placed on her son's army career, destroyed it to frustrate her sister's predictable ambitions. The only certainties, however, are Vasilisa Kashporovna's suspicion that Storchenko has purloined the deed and her hope of recovering it with her nephew's aid. Such is the task for which she now prepares him by apprising him of the benefits that would surely accrue and by boosting his confidence with her lavish praise, and her efforts, it seems, are not in vain. Not only does Shpon'ka accede to her wishes; he even sets forth on his delicate mission in the trap that she uses for "the shooting of game" (296).

By this time, however, it is already well known to the reader that Vasilisa Kashporovna's choice of game is as ill-conceived as her choice of hunter. The evidence is the portrait of Storchenko in chapter 2 which describes the hero's meeting with him at an inn in the course of his journey home, for the portrait not only precedes that of Vasilisa Kashporovna; it also prefigures it, presenting another, directly comparable blend of the same "masculine" symbols that were later to form the basis of the portraits of Sobakevich and Nozdryov. Once more the name is worthy of note, for in addition to comprising another composite allusion to quintessential masculine characteristics, its components directly parallel those of Vasilisa Kashporovna in respect of their Greek and Ukrainian sources. Thus while the Christian name and patronymic, which have their source in the Greek verb *grēgorein* ("to be awake"), implicitly attribute him with the vitality and vigour which are the mark of all Gogol's "masculine" creations and indirectly explain his departure from the inn "before dawn" (291), i.e. before Shpon'ka has risen, the surname, derived from the Ukrainian adverb *storch* ("sternly"), proclaims at once the authoritarian strain in his "Sobakevichan" personality, merely reiterating, in effect, the narrator's earlier reference to him as "a stern interrogator" (*strogiy doproschik*) (290).[16] Neither the corpulent physique, therefore, that he shares with Sobakevich and Vasilisa Kashporovna,[17] nor the reappearance in his portrait of the "military" and "hunting" motifs gives cause for surprise. While the name of his estate "Khortyshche" is derived from *khort*, which means "a hunting greyhound", the effect of his voice on Shpon'ka, we read, is such that the hero "involuntarily rose from his seat and stood at attention, as he usually did when the colonel asked him a question" (290). Thus the conclusion suggested by these details is clearly that in the figure of Storchenko Gogol was intent on creating a direct male counterpart to the hero's masculine aunt, a fitting masculine adversary, and it is in this connection, of course, that we must consider his marital status. Just as Vasilisa Kashporovna is a spinster, i.e. a hater of males, so Storchenko is a bachelor, i.e. a hater of females, and it may be noted in reference to this point that even before he appears physically in the story his misogyny is clearly evoked, for his "loud voice," in the narrator's words, is heard "quarrelling with the old woman who kept the inn". It announces: "I will drive in, but if a single bug bites me in your inn, I will beat you, I swear I will beat you, you old witch!" (289). And even when he falls asleep, he still contrives to torment the poor woman — not coincidentally, we may perhaps assume, with his nose. He "filled the room," we read, "with a terrible nasal whistle, snoring so loudly at times that the old woman, who was dozing on the stove-bench, suddenly woke up and stared about her wide-eyed, but seeing nothing she calmed down and fell asleep again" (292). By thus endowing Storchenko from the beginning with the characteristic misogyny of his masculine males, Gogol prepares the way for the ensuing conflict.

At this point, however, we must temporarily switch our attention to a different conflict — namely, to that in which Storchenko is already engaged, for the description of Shpon'ka's visit to Khortyshche reveals that he is already embroiled in sexual warfare. Perceiving at once behind Shpon'ka's story of the legacy the vigorous prompting of his rapacious aunt, Storchenko naturally dismisses it as a tissue of lies. But there is another threat to his position that he cannot so easily dismiss. Although only six months have passed since he succeeded his uncle, he already displays a form of physical discomfort which immediately relates him to every other male in Gogol's fiction who is similarly threatened by a female assault. When Shpon'ka encounters him, he is portrayed "walking about the yard in his frock-coat, but without his tie, his waistcoat and his braces", and the narrator continues: "It seemed, however, that even this attire weighed oppressively on his corpulent person, for the perspiration was streaming from him" (297). Again, of course, no ulterior level of meaning suggests itself at first sight. Even in the absence of any reference to hot weather, it does not seem curious that a man of Storchenko's dimensions should perspire freely while walking or even, perhaps, that he should have shed his braces. What does seem a little curious is simply that Gogol should mention the fact and accumulate the details in this way, i.e. until we remember the indicated implications in his works of the metaphor of heat and of the metaphorical culinary skills of his masculinized females. The portrait of the perspiring, half-stripped Storchenko directly prefigures the experience of Chichikov, who as Koroboch-ka's guest is first prevailed on to surrender his wet clothes, then subjected in bed to the intolerable heat of her enormous quilts (VI, 47), and finally reduced by her obstinacy to a state of such exasperation that "he was covered all over with sweat, as if he had fallen into a river; everything that he was wearing, from his shirt to his stockings, was wet" (VI, 55). Storchenko's cry: "It's so hot here that my whole shirt is wet" (297) expresses the same symbolic discomfort, the characteristic anguish inflicted on the Gogolian male by the masculinized Gogolian female.

On his first appearance, therefore, in his own domain Storchenko is portrayed in the process of being "steamed" or "stewed", and the source of the heat is quickly revealed. Although, like Vasilisa Kashporovna, he is a newcomer who appears to have assumed total control, it is soon made clear that he has immeasurably more formidable obstacles to overcome than a passive nephew — namely, a family that is exclusively female and a mother who is renowned as a cook. The major interest, in fact, of chapter 4, which is mainly devoted to the description of the dinner held in Shpon'ka's honour, lies precisely in its allusions to the sexual war within the Storchenko family. Here the presence of Shpon'ka serves merely as a stimulus to renewed hostilities between mother and son. Initially the conflict is conveyed in a relatively direct manner, for example, by Storchenko's sharp reproof of his mother for enquiring whether the guest has had a drink of vodka instead of simply offering him one. "You merely offer it to us," he exclaims. "Whether we have drunk any or not is our business" (298). Thus the line between the sexes is drawn at once: the function of the female, the reproof implies, is to serve the male, and that is all. Rather more oblique, however, and distinctly more characteristic of the mature Gogol are the symbolic indications of the conflict that he inserts at this juncture by introducing the female of a different species — namely, the turkey-hen that is consumed at dinner. The device anticipates the numerous examples of similar transitions in the later tales which are likewise designed to reflect the sexual conflicts between the characters. Particularly noteworthy is the hasty intervention of Storchenko's mother to deter Shpon'ka from sampling an unseemly part of the bird's anatomy. "You are wrong," she cries, "to take the bishop's nose, Ivan Fyodorovich. It's a turkey-hen! Take the back!" (299). Unless we again take the view that Gogol's aim here is simply to amuse, only one interpretation would seem to be possible — that the entreaty is a plea for respect of the female, a desperate attempt to defend female honour, even though the female in question be only a roasted bird. And the vehement riposte of the misogynistic Storchenko would seem to support this reading. Evidently impatient for the dishonour to be inflicted, he interjects: "Mother! No one is asking you to interfere! You may be sure that our guest knows what to take himself!" And we note that far from restricting his fellow male to the bishop's nose, he spurs him on to take a leg, a wing and finally the gizzard, thus implicitly inviting him to share his own delight in the mutilation of the female.

The roasted, mutilated hen, in short, may be regarded as symbolic of the condition to which Storchenko aspires to reduce the females of his household.[18] But their actual condition, of course, is quite different, as is confirmed both by his own "roasted", perspiring condition and by the meaningful juxtaposition in Shpon'ka's report on his visit to his aunt which seems to remove all doubt about the hen's symbolic role: "There was also a turkey-hen! ... Very handsome young ladies — Grigory Grigor'yevich's sisters, especially the fair one" (302). Not for nothing, we may assume, is Storchenko compared by the narrator, as he sits draped with his napkin at the head of the table, to "the heroes depicted by barbers on their signboards" (299). Having already illuminated the danger that threatens his position with the motif of "stripping", Gogol now switches in characteristic fashion to a cognate motif to reassert the point, introducing the motif of shaving that was later to serve as his principal symbol of emasculation in "The Nose". And as if to signal the weakening of the masculine vitality denoted by Storchenko's Christian name and patronymic, he duly consigns him after his gestures of defiance to a post-prandial sleep. The concatenation of motifs points unmistakably to the eventual outcome of the sexual conflict. Surrounded by three females and two emasculated males — Shpon'ka and the loquacious Ivan Ivanovich, whose subservience to female power may be inferred from the distinction that he draws between his own fat turkey-hens and the "skinny" specimen on the table (299-300) — the master of Khortyshche is engaged in a lonely and losing battle, and even as he sleeps, his fate is assiduously plotted by his vengeful attendant "cooks". In his absence the old lady, far from displaying any inclination to sleep herself, "became more talkative," we read, "and of her own accord, without being asked, revealed many secrets about the making of fruit fudge and the drying of pears" (301), i.e. about the destruction of "sweet" souls.

Naturally enough, the state of affairs at Khortyshche is immediately deduced by the perceptive Vasilisa Kashporovna from her nephew's account of his experiences. Her instinctive reaction, of course, to the news that Storchenko disclaims all knowledge of the deed of gift is to brandish the weapon of her "terrible hand". "I'll get rid of some of his fat for him," she cries (302), thus threatening him with his own treatment of his "skinny" turkey-hen. But Shpon'-ka's confirmation that the old lady's vaunted culinary skills are still undiminished, combined with his favourable reference to Storchenko's fair-haired sister, convinces her that a violent intrusion would be quite superfluous. While the task of "roasting" her adversary can clearly be left to his domestic "cooks", the "dowel" can now perform his most useful service. By effecting the union to which his name alludes, he can now ensure her eventual triumph. Undeterred by his horror at the prospect of marriage, she prepares for the visit that will secure the match, and in the deceptive form of an apparent digression her fundamental preoccupation is disclosed once more. Commenting on her "majestic chaise", the narrator observes:

> I consider it my duty to inform the reader that it was the same chaise in which Adam once rode; and therefore, if anyone tries to pass off another as Adam's, it is a downright lie and his chaise is certainly a fake. It is quite unknown how it survived the Flood. It must be supposed that in Noah's Ark there was a special coach-house for it (303-4).

By her possession of Adam's carriage Vasilisa Kashporovna is not only related here to the first female to cause a male's fall from grace; she is identified as the very incarnation of the age-old female drive to usurp the male's dominant position, and it seems fitting that even the structure of the chaise should reflect the same drive. "The chaise was constructed," the narrator continues, "a little on one side, so that its right side was much higher than the left, and this pleased her immensely because, as she put it, a short person could climb up on one side and a tall person on the other" (304). It need hardly be remarked that the terms "short person" and "tall person" are respectively synonymous here with "male" and "female". Despite the greater weight of Vasilisa Kashporovna and the absence of any reference in the tale to Shpon'ka's shortness, it is predictably the aunt who occupies the higher right-hand position when the time for departure eventually arrives. Once more Gogol uses the generic endings of Russian to point the sexual contrast: "Ivan Fyodorovich and his aunt boarded the carriage, one (*odin*) from the left side, the other (*drugaya*) from the right . . ." (304).

Providing, therefore, yet another indication that Gogol's alleged digressions are often important vehicles of his symbolic central theme, the narrator's comments on the heroine's carriage may clearly be taken to mark the transition to a decisive stage in the sexual conflict. Once more the female triumph is obliquely predicted, and it seems no coincidence that when the visitors arrive "Grigory Grigor'yevich was not at home" (304). Here Gogol contrives for the first time to create the illusion that repeatedly strikes the reader of his tales — the illusion that the daughters of Eve are uncannily united in an act of vengeful, conspiratorial collusion. Never before have the female neighbours met, yet not only do the females of Khortyshche seem to have sensed in advance their ally's arrival and to have ensured that the enemy is absent at the appointed time; they also address her, in the narrator's words, "as if they had known one another all their lives". By such means Gogol evokes the impression of an instinctive, concerted female resolve directly comparable to that which ensures Chichikov's failure in the later chapters of *Dead Souls*, and in the symbolic form of the ladies' subject of conversation — "the pickling of cucumbers and the drying of pears" (305) — he reveals the sinister task to which they are jointly devoted.

From this subject the old lady and her formidable guest pass directly and logically to the means of achieving their aim — to discussion of the union that will cement their alliance — and before he realises that his fate is sealed, Shpon'ka finds himself alone with the fair-haired Masha, who is ominously attributed with eyebrows reminiscent of those of Vasilisa Kashporovna in her youth (302) and has evidently experienced, to judge from her age (twenty-five), similar difficulty in attracting suitors. For fifteen minutes not a word is exchanged, and as comic as the silence which conveys Shpon'ka's paralysis is the one inept remark that he contrives to produce: "There are a great many flies in summer, Miss" (305). Yet even here, in this celebrated observation, we seem to encounter the familiar tension between levels of meaning. Once more there is good reason to believe that the "surface" is deceptive, that the comic appearance masks the presence of significant symbols. Thus while the reference to summer may be taken as an extension of the metaphor of heat (anticipating the narrator's comment on the hero as he later reflects on his dire predicament: "The more he sank into thought, the more the sweat stood out on his face" (307)), the reference to the flies introduces the image that was later to be used to characterise the oppressed position of the hero of "The Overcoat" (III, 143, 169) and to symbolise the fate of the spider-like Korobochka's male victims.[19] Examined in the light of these symbols, Shpon'ka's observation presents itself less as a mark of ineptitude than as an anguished lament — a lament on the fate inflicted on the male of the species which relates his own position not only to the common dilemma of the "sons of Adam" but, more pertinently, to the particular dilemma of his perspiring host which is the primary concern of the assembled females. And regarded as a response to this lament, Masha's reply may be seen to be entirely apt, for it expresses precisely the relation of the general to the particular. She remarks: "A very great many! My dear brother (*bratets*) has purposely made a swotter out of an old shoe (*bashmaka*) of mother's" (305). Thus from the general multitude of flies she passes to the individual "fly" who by his defiant self-assertion has converted his mother into the "swotter" that will destroy him. Like the "Promethean" husband of Korobochka, the "Prometheus" of Khortyshche is seemingly condemned to be reduced to the status of a fly and squashed under a female boot.[20] In Masha's reply Gogol provides us with one of our first glimpses not only of his characteristically ambivalent use of diminutives (for the literal meaning of *bratets* is "*little brother*"), but also of yet another symbol of female oppression that he was later to use with telling effect — the image of the female shoe (*bashmak*) which, like the image of the fly, was to play a more prominent role in his most famous study of a "downtrodden" male: that of the clerk named Bashmachkin.[21]

But the story of Storchenko is now discontinued. Its end is prefigured and its role is exhausted — namely, that of proclaiming that under the combined assault of swotter, heat and shoe even the most masculine of males is doomed to succumb. It remains only to convey the pain of final submission as now experienced by the impotent hero, and this is achieved in the concluding two pages by evoking the female invasion of his disintegrating mind. The process commences with his bombardment by "noise". When the sentence of marriage is duly confirmed, "Ivan Fyodorovich," we read, "stood as though deafened by thunder" (306), and yet again we are reminded of Chichikov's arrival at Korobochka's estate — of the claps of thunder, the barking hounds and the stunning clock which in rapid succession assail his ears (VI, 44-6). In both cases noise seems to symbolise the female assault on the male's senses and vitality[22] and thus motivates the transition to the motif of sleep which is used, as we have noted, to mark Storchenko's weakening. While Chichikov feels that "his eyes had stuck, as if someone had smeared them with honey" (VI, 45) and immediately retires to the bed that awaits him, Shpon'ka, we are told, "went to bed earlier than usual" (307).[23]

But whereas Chichikov is blissfully unaware of his perilous position and consequently lapses into peaceful repose, the sleep of Shpon'ka is rent by female spectres. From every side in the world of his dreams, while "everything around him was whirling with noise", he is assailed by "wives" in bizarre disguises, and prominent among them is logically his aunt — the arbiter of his fate and embodiment of his conception of the female personality. Here the device of dream is used by Gogol both to associate the notion of a wife with the masculine persecutors of Shpon'ka's personal experience — not only with Vasilisa Kashporovna, but also with his regimental colonel and the Latin master who, like one of the "wives", once "seized him by the ear" (285, 307) — and also to generate new metaphors of the masculinized female which, like so many other elements of this seminal work, were later to be pressed into effective service: for example, the images of the goose and belfry, that were to reappear in *Dead Souls* in the portrait of Sobakevich's wife,[24] and the image of "the coat" (introduced by the noun *syurtuk* ("frock-coat")), which was again to acquire uxorial connotations in "The Overcoat". In the context of "Shpon'ka" Gogol provides no logical explanation for these images, and indeed any attempt to explain them would be patently out of place. Their function, both individually and collectively, is merely to evoke a vivid impression of the breakdown of logic in the hero's mind. They are simply accumulated, therefore, and left suspended in the dream-world from which they were later to be transferred to the more "explanatory" contexts of different conceptions. But there is one recurrent image in the sequence which, as we have seen, is fully explained within "Shpon'ka" itself: the thrice repeated image of the hero bathed in perspiration. Introducing the reader for the first time in the tale to the fully developed symbolic system that he had devised to express his allegorical theme of sexual conflict, Gogol appropriately concludes the work by reiterating the image that was henceforth to epitomise the male's invariable predicament.

The repetition of the image not only re-emphasizes what is already apparent — namely, that the conclusion of the narrative is the logical outcome of everything that has gone before; it also marks the end of the story of the hero in the sense that it clearly foreshadows his fate. Its effect, therefore, is to confront us with one of the major problems posed by the tale: why, if the story of the hero is essentially complete, does Gogol create the impression that the narrative is unfinished and entrust to Rudyy Pan'ko a detailed and comic explanation of the fact? The answer most commonly given is that he is simply amusing himself here with the conventions of narrative form, displaying, as Setchkarev and others have argued, his susceptibility to the influence of Sterne.[25] But there is also another possible answer, which gains in plausibility from the fact that it relates the unfinished state of the narrative directly to the story's theme (as we have interpreted it). If we examine the Foreword in the light of this theme, we will see that the generally accepted explanation is almost as misleading as the equally popular view to which Setchkarev also subscribes — that the plot of the tale "is of rather secondary interest".[26] "To analyze the plot of *Dead Souls*," writes Andrey Belyy, "means to ignore the fiction of the fable and to grasp the small details which have absorbed both the fable and the plot . . . There is no plot in *Dead Souls* apart from the details; it must be squeezed from them."[27] Having "squeezed" the details of "Shpon'ka", we have seen that its plot is likewise inseparable from the details and that, far from being "of secondary interest", it embraces the entire narrative section, including the numerous details that seem to shoot off at tangents. Similarly, if we "squeeze" the details of the Foreword, we will see that it too is embraced by the plot and, moreover, that it constitutes, in effect, the plot's genuine conclusion — a conclusion that follows logically from the ensuing narrative. We will see, in other words, that the story of Shpon'ka is left hanging because its clearly indicated dénouement does not conclude Gogol's development of his theme.

The argument thus far has been that, recording the submission of one male and the imminent submission of another to female domination, the story is essentially an exposé of the female drive to usurp the male's position. The narrator's sex, therefore, is not irrelevant, for the task of exposure would presumably be assumed only by a male who is fully conscious of the danger and intent on sounding the alarm. Such, it seems, is Stepan Ivanovich Kurochka, and the editor's apparently gratuitous information about him in the Foreword fully confirms this interpretation of his reason for undertaking the task. It reveals that, like Shpon'ka and Storchenko, Stepan Ivanovich is under attack. Even his surname, which means "little hen" is perhaps meant, like the image of the dead male quail (*perepel*) on the pole outside his house (284),[28] to allude to the fact, reminding us not only of Storchenko's mutilated turkey-hen but also of the fate of hens, and birds generally, in Korobochka's domain.[29] But all doubt is removed by the editor's disclosure that although Stepan Ivanovich is a bachelor, visitors to his house are met by a "stout woman" wearing a "green skirt" (284), i.e. a skirt the same colour as Storchenko's frock-coat (289). Once more the idea of surveillance is introduced. The bachelor seems obliged to conduct his life under the surveillance of a female who is linked by her corpulence and apparel with the two main embodiments in the tale of the masculine attributes. But although an obvious affinity is thus established between narrator and hero, Stepan Ivanovich is plainly no passive tool. Not only is his bachelor status still intact, but, like his female watchdog, he also display affinities with both Storchenko and Vasilisa Kashporovna. Thus, like Storchenko, he is given to rising early in the morning,[30] and he earns himself the nickname "windmill" by his habit of "swinging his arms as he walks" (284) — a peculiarity that may be regarded as similarly alluding to his masculine vitality in the light both of the reference fourteen lines later to Shpon'ka's habit of sitting at school "with his arms folded" and of the spectacle that heralds the appearance of Vasilisa Kashporovna when Shpon'ka returns to his estate: that of "the windmill waving its sails" (292). By such means the point is conveyed that Stepan Ivanovich is still defiant.

But the principal evidence, of course, of his continuing refusal to submit is his tale, his graphic exposé of the female craving for power, and we may now appreciate not only why the tale is largely composed in a symbolic code, but also why, instead of being recounted orally before the usual mixed audience, it is told only to the editor (a fellow male) and, at the latter's request, committed to paper. The implication is that, on hearing the tale, Rudyy Pan'ko fully recognized its purpose and its unsuitability for oral rendering. Hence his concealment of the manuscript in his "little table". But, like every other male in Gogol's works, he seriously underestimates the female's resolve, her instinctive capacity for detecting rebellion. Although he insists that his wife is illiterate, his praise of her cooking predicts the manuscript's fate. Like Shpon'ka and Storchenko, it is subjected to heat, thrust page by page with her pies into the oven, and only half of it is left when the disaster is discovered.

Remarkably, therefore, the tale itself, as a manifestation of male rebellion, suffers the punishment inflicted on its heroes. Yet clearly the important point is less the similarity of the punishment than the difference of the outcome – the survival of a half of the tale that fully reflects Stepan Ivanovich's purpose – for its survival can only be interpreted as his victory and, as such, as a vital element of the story's plot. In other words, the very existence of the story of male defeat paradoxically represents a male victory, and in the final reckoning this victory, the victory of the narrator, may be seen to be the essential point of the tale and to form its actual conclusion. In one sense, therefore, Stepan Ivanovich may legitimately be viewed as the story's real hero. But in the light of this interpretation it is clear that an equally strong claim to this status can be made by the male who ensures his victory – Rudyy Pan'ko, who not only rescued the surviving half of the manuscript but even reproduced it for the reader's benefit despite his attested awareness of its "dangerous" import. Expressing his reaction to his wife's assault on the manuscript, the editor remarks: "It would be silly to fight (*podrat'sya*) at our time of life!" (283), but the Russian verb refers primarily to physical "fighting"; his refusal to *drat'sya* does not exclude the more subtle form of combat represented by the publication of the surviving half of the manuscript. Rudyy Pan'ko, in short, *does* fight, using the manuscript as his weapon, and thereby he reveals not only a salient feature of his personality, but also, perhaps, the major purpose of the entire volume that he has edited, for the evidence that he is using one story to expose the female's campaign against the male at least raises the question of whether the others were not included with the same object in view.

The editor's other extensive interventions in *Evenings* – the Forewords to the two Parts of the volume – certainly provide additional grounds for supposing that this may well be the case, i.e. that the purpose (and implicitly the theme) of "Shpon'ka" is at least a major purpose (and implicitly a major theme) of the volume as a whole. In the context, for example, of his opening remarks in the Foreword to Part One, which convey his apprehension about the reception that will be accorded the volume, Rudyy Pan'ko makes the following striking statement:

> ... for a villager like me to poke his nose out of his hole into the great world – good gracious (*batyushki moi*)! It's just like what happens sometimes when you enter the rooms of a great lord: they all surround you and make you feel like a fool (103).

Perhaps the first point to note is the ambiguity of the exclamation *batyushki moi*, for its literal meaning is not "good gracious" but "my dear fellows", suggesting that its meaning as an interjection is conceivably the mask of a specific address to the male readership which would plainly harmonize with the hypothesis that it is for the benefit of males that the volume has been compiled. But rather more significant is the early intrusion of the image of the nose, which suggests that Rudyy Pan'ko's timidity is less that of a self-conscious editor than that of a male stepping nervously into a hostile world. For if the image of the nose is taken here, as Gogol's fiction in its entirety suggests it must be, to possess the symbolic sexual connotations that have been attributed to it, then the phrase "the great world" must likewise be attributed with a more specific meaning than appearances would indicate, denoting the female-dominated world into which Gogolian noses (as symbols of male masculinity) are poked at their peril. Nor is this interpretation incompatible with the indirect comparison of "the great world" to "the rooms of a great lord (*velikogo pana*)", for the position and sexual attributes of Gogol's female usurpers, as the name and portrait of Vasilisa Kashporovna have demonstrated, are indeed those of "a great lord", while the position of his heroes is at best that of a "little lord" (*pan'ko*). The name Pan'ko, in reality, is a diminutive of the Christian name Panteleymon, but there can be little doubt that it is no less meaningful here than the names of the characters of "Shpon'ka". Suggesting the notion of "little lord" and contrasting with the noun *pan* in the quoted statement, it may be taken to allude to the female usurpation of masculine authority both in "the great world" into which the editor launches his volume and in the more limited world of his personal household, while the nickname Rudyy ("Ginger"), together with the Foreword to "Shpon'ka", would seem to explain this reversal of conventional sexual roles. Just as the "ginger whiskers" (*ryzhiye usiki*) of Nozdryov's brother-in-law Mizhuyev (VI, 63) have been "singed" by the "hunter's" rifle-like chibouk,[31] so the editor of *Evenings*, we may deduce, like the manuscript of "Shpon'ka", has been "singed" in the kitchen of his personal "great lord", to whose culinary skills he pays such lavish and meaningful tribute whenever he apostrophizes his (male) readers.[32]

The conclusion, therefore, that is prompted by these details is that the anxiety of Rudyy Pan'ko, like that of the narrator of *Dead Souls* (VI, 223), has its source in the likely reaction of the female reader to his volume, and this explanation, of course, significantly strengthens the argument that his purpose in publishing "Shpon'ka", as we have defined it, is relevant to the volume as a whole. In addition, it would suggest that the structure of the volume is also meaningful, that an element of astuteness is to be detected in Rudyy Pan'ko's consistent refusal to pass off the tales as his own, for by attributing their authorship to their various narrators — who, unlike Pushkin's narrators in *The Tales of Belkin* (*Povesti Belkina*), are all male — he plainly insures himself to some degree against a violent female riposte. This does not mean, of course, that the narrators have been simply created by the editor for his self-protection, for such an assumption would obviously founder on the sharp differences of style between the tales. It merely implies that the two principal narrators, like Stepan Ivanovich Kurochka, are united with the editor in a common purpose which he is more inclined to attribute to them than to himself.

His introductory remarks on these two narrators are just as revealing in this respect as the information that he imparts about Stepan Ivanovich. Thus the sacristan of the Dikan'ka church, Foma Grigor'yevich, is endowed not only with Storchenko's expressive patronymic, but also with a conspicuous concern for the welfare of his nose, i.e. for the preservation of his masculine identity. The editor reports:

> No one would say that he ever wiped his nose with the flap of his overall, as other men of his calling do; he would take from his bosom a neatly folded white handkerchief embroidered round the edges with red cotton, and after putting it to its proper use, he would fold it up again in twelve, as was his custom, and put it back in his bosom (105).

And the editor adds later, understandably disguising with adjective and adverb his unqualified admiration of the sacristan's masculine habits: "A certain dignity shines on his face, *even* when he takes a pinch of ordinary snuff; *even* then you feel an *involuntary* respect for him" (197).[33] Equally eloquent details are likewise apparent in the portrait of the other major narrator, the "fine young gentlemen" (alias "little lord" (*panich*)) from Poltava. He too is linked with Storchenko, like Stepan Ivanovich's female attendant, by the colour of his attire (his "pea-green caftan") and, like the sacristan, parades his masculinity by elaborately feeding his nose on generous pinches of snuff (105-6) and by "holding it high in the air" (196). Moreover, he even has the temerity to criticise the methods of pickling espoused by Rudyy Pan'ko's wife, taking umbrage and scornfully departing when the nervous editor attempts to restrain him (196). Like the "windmill' Stepan Ivanovich, in short, the two narrators indirectly convey the purpose of their tales by proudly exhibiting the masculine characteristics which the editor himself is anxious to conceal, and the experience of Foma Grigor'yevich confirms his wisdom. "Our village roads," Rudyy Pan'ko informs us, "are not as smooth as those that pass in front of your mansions. The year before last Foma Grigor'yevich, as he was driving here from Dikan'ka, fell into a ditch with his new gig and bay mare, even though he was driving himself and occasionally donned his spectacles" (106-7). The concluding concessive clause effectively masks the statement of cause. Like the approaches to Korobochka's estate, the roads leading to and from Dikan'ka are clearly a snare for the unwary male excessively preoccupied with the well-being of his nose, and the overturning of the sacristan's gig duly foreshadows the "nosey" Chichikov's[34] tumble in Korobochka's mud (VI, 42). Not for nothing, it seems, does the name "Dikan'ka" evoke with its feminine gender and root-element *dik-* ("wild") the idea of "ferocious woman". Not for nothing is the village described by the editor as excelling in certain respects St. Petersburg itself (106), the symbolic, female-dominated St. Petersburg in which, as we shall see, the action of "The Nose" and

"The Overcoat" was to be set. The symbolic capital of the later tales has its prototype in this symbolic Ukrainian village and the "sleep-inducing" Mirgorod ("Peaceville") in which the male asserts himself at the risk of his life. Hence the preference of Rudyy Pan'ko, whose household is plainly a microcosm of the village, for the more subtle form of self-assertion represented by the editing of his colleagues' tales. "If you show yourself," he declares, "you must face the consequences" (103), but at least he "shows himself" with commendable guile.

Although, however, our hypothesis concerning the purpose of the volume receives support from the portraits of the principal narrators, it must ultimately be tested, of course, against the evidence of their tales. We must now ascertain in other words, whether the psychological affinities with Stepan Ivanovich revealed by the symbolic details in their portraits are matched by similar affinities between their stories. Certainly the initial impression produced by the differences of period, setting, atmosphere and style is that little is to be gained from the exercise, yet it does not require a particularly close examination to see that significant affinities do exist and that the differences — particularly those of style — can easily be exaggerated. Indeed, it soon becomes apparent that both the allegorical theme of "Shpon'ka" and the symbolic system devised to express it are repeatedly in evidence.

The most obvious testimony to this fact is clearly the recurrence and prominence in the tales of variations of the image of the masculinized female. Usually cast in the role of stepmothers or sisters-in-law, they not only remind us repeatedly of Vasilisa Kashporovna but highlight, in effect, the evolutionary process through which the image passed before acquiring in her portrait, as it were, its final, mature form. From the beginning familiar motifs are employed to create the image. Thus the tyrannical Khivrya in the first of the tales, "The Sorochintsy Fair", which is evidently narrated by the *panich* in the pea-green caftan, sports a "green jacket", a cap that gives her "a particularly majestic air", a "savage" (*dikoye*) expression on her face, and a patronymic of Greek derivation (Nikiforovna) which signifies "victorious in battle" (113). In addition, she displays her "military" capabilities by assaulting the hero, Grits'ko, with "a sharp volley (*zalpom*) of unexpected greetings" (114) and is credited by the priest's son for her culinary skills with "the cleverest pair of hands of any daughter of Eve" (123). Similarly the wife of the sacristan in "Christmas Eve" is endowed with a "terrible hand" (*strashnoyu rukoyu*) (218), while the wife of Panas in the same tale "fought (*dralas'*) only in the mornings with her husband," we read, "as it was only then that she sometimes saw him. . . . Despite his habitual composure he did not like to yield to her, and consequently left the house almost every day with both eyes blackened" (228). "O Lord," cries Solopy Cherevik in "The Sorochintsy Fair", as his "formidable spouse" (122) Khivrya ominously advances on him, "why hast Thou visited such a misfortune on us sinners? With so many unpleasant things in the world, Thou has gone and created women!" (120).

Like most of the males in these stories, Solopy is a Cossack — a name synonymous with daring, defiance and pugnacity, with all the multiplicity of quintessentially masculine attributes — yet his cry is echoed throughout the volume, highlighting the familiar inversion of conventional sexual roles. "Call yourselves Cossacks and men!" taunts Khivrya. "You're nothing but a lot of women!" (126). It is true that not every Cossack is so pathetically submissive. Even Solopy is capable of occasional masculine, military gestures, of "waving his arms (like a "windmill" — J.B.W.), as though beating a drum", almost "grazing Khivrya's face" (129-30), while Grits'ko goes so far as to proclaim: "If I were the Tsar or a great lord (*panom velikim*), I would be the first to hang all those fools who let themselves be saddled by women" (121). But with only one obvious exception, the "great lords" in the volume are exclusively female. Only Danilo Burul'bash in "A Terrible Vengeance" (*Strashnaya mest'*) asserts his authority as Cossack and male, and even he is brought low by the evil in his wife's family. "Be silent, woman!" he commands her. "Whoever gets mixed up with you will turn into a woman himself. . . . A Cossack, thank God, fears neither devils nor Catholic priests. What should we come to if we started obeying our wives — eh, my lads? Our wife is a pipe and a sharp sabre!" (247).[35]

Perhaps the most significant feature of this tirade is the oblique association that it establishes between the female and the principle of evil ("devils"). Not only is it repeated later in the tale, when Danilo, unaware that his wife has released her father from his cell, attributes the act to the devil (264), but it is progressively reinforced, with characteristic Gogolian virtuosity, from the first page of the volume to the last. "There's the devil in my old woman!" says Solopy Cherevik (133), thus echoing Grits'ko's earlier reference to Khivrya: "There in front sits the devil!" (114), while in "Christmas Eve" the phrase "diabolical woman" (*chortova baba*) is applied by Panas to his wife (229) and by Chub to the temptress Solokha (231). The importance of the point, however, is not confined to the corroborative light that it casts on the moral implications of Gogol's female portraits; it also sheds additional light on the logic behind his "details". It explains, for example, why Khivrya's green jacket is "adorned with little tails" (113) and why she is so intent on acquiring over the priest's son the kind of influence that Korobochka later wields over her associate Father Kiril.[36] It may also explain why one of Gogol's misogynistic narrators is the sacristan of the Dikan'ka church and why Stepan Ivanovich Kurochka not only lives "near the brick church" but is to be found every morning before nine o'clock conversing with "Father Antip" (284). And most important of all, it reveals the origins of the related motifs which are reflected in Khivrya's means of achieving her aim — the motifs of "cooking" and "heat" which play, as we have seen already, such a central role in Gogol's symbolic system. Thus referring to the devil, the narrator of "Christmas Eve" observes:

... it's no wonder that he should be cold, being accustomed day after day to knocking about in hell, where, as is well known, it is not as cold as it is here in winter, and where, donning his cap and standing before the hearth just like a cook, he fries sinners with as much pleasure as a woman usually displays when frying sausage at Christmas (210).

Once more the comedy is plainly a facade concealing the implications of the concluding simile. Relating Gogol's female cooks to the "cook" in hell, the simile implicitly equates the emasculation of the Gogolian male with the destruction of a soul. It equates the perspiring Shpon'ka and Storchenko with the deluded Petro in "St. John's Eve" (*Vecher nakanune Ivana Kupala*), whose reward for succumbing to the witch's temptations is to be reduced, like Korobochka's blacksmith (VI, 51), to "a heap of ashes from which here and there smoke (*par*) was still rising" (150).

It is hardly surprising, therefore, that in the folkish world of *Evenings* the disguise of witch is the most common of the guises in which the masculinized female presents herself, and again it is to this early form of characterisation that elements of the later portraits may repeatedly be traced — most notably, perhaps, the image of the cat, which recurs in the portraits of the witch in "St. John's Eve", the stepmother in "A May Night" (*Mayskaya noch'*) and Solokha in "Christmas Eve". Is it coincidental, for example, that Masha, during her "mute scene" with Shpon'ka, is so preoccupied with the movements of a cat under the chairs (305) and that a cat plays such an important part in the life of Pul'kheriya Ivanovna in "Old-World Landowners"? Is it mere chance that Storchenko addresses the old woman at the inn as "you old witch" (289) and responds to Shpon'ka's enquiry about the deed of gift by charging his aunt with having "cast a spell" (*nagovorit'*) on him (297)? And is it again coincidence, given the habit of the witches in "The Lost Letter" (*Propavshaya gramota*) of riding not on broomsticks but on pokers (185), that it is with a poker that Panas is beaten by his wife in "Christmas Eve" (229) and that Vasilisa Kashporovna brandishes a poker at the dogs that steal her pies (303)? These details surely provide a clear indication that the masculinized female, as portrayed in "Shpon'ka", and subsequently in *Mirgorod*, the "Petersburg tales" and *Dead Souls*, is related directly to the witches of Gogol's first volume, to the daughters of the "infernal cook".

Even on the basis, therefore, of this brief survey of character-types and recurrent details it can be asserted that, contrary to the general view, "Shpon'ka" is not thematically exceptional in the context of *Evenings*. Indeed, a more lengthy survey would show that in all of the other seven stories (though only episodically, it seems, in "A Place Bewitched" (*Zakoldovannoye mesto*) (315)) males are similarly the victims of violence or evil forces associated with females, confirming that the common purpose ascribed to the editor and narrators is reflected in the volume as a whole. It may be objected, of course, that, despite the sufferings of Solopy, we still leave hero and heroine in "The Sorochintsy Fair" locked in happy embrace, but do we not detect in the concluding paragraphs ominous forebodings of Grits'ko's future — in Khivrya's assaults on the protective wall of dancers, in the depressing portrait of the witch-like old women, and in the narrator's lament on the transience of joy (135-6)? And although Vakula appears likewise to find happiness in the arms of Oksana in "Christmas Eve", the central symbol of the tale, as our study of "The Overcoat" will show, discloses the truth behind the deceptive appearance.[37] Only Levko, in fact, in "A May Night" seems to enjoy an unqualified triumph and may accordingly be regarded, together with Stepan Ivanovich Kurochka, as a lonely precursor of the few males who prevail in Gogol's later volumes.

It is clear, however, that the links between "Shpon'ka" and the other tales are not only thematic. The importance of the comparison lies equally in the evidence that it provides of the continuity of Gogol's narrative art, of the essential homogeneity of his fictional universe, for it is now apparent that the traditional devices and stock figures of the folk-tale are not so much abandoned in "Shpon'ka" and the later stories as adapted to the creation of a more realistic-looking symbolic reality which expresses a moral judgment on the Russia of Gogol's own time. Neither the witch, as we have seen, nor the devil disappears after the folkish tales of *Evenings* and *Mirgorod*; they are merely transplanted from the folk-tale world of these volumes and clothed anew in the attire of nineteenth-century Russian citizens, in which they continue to display both their moral significance and their fictional origins. Similarly the traditional folk-tale device of "abrupt, unmotivated metamorphosis", which Erlich has described as "the leitmotif of *Evenings*",[38] continues to be used just as extensively in "Shpon'ka" and the later fiction as in the other tales of *Evenings* and "Viy", merely undergoing the changes of form and function required for the creation of a more "realistic" illusion. Thus in "St. John's Eve", for example, it is explicitly stated that the witch changes into a cat and "a large black dog" (145), but it is not stated in chapter 3 of *Dead Souls* that Korobochka changes into the strutting turkey-cock that denotes her sexual metamorphosis (VI, 48).[39] We are simply confronted with the image and left to infer from the details woven into the description of the cock that Korobochka is the referent.[40] The explicit metamorphosis, in short, of the folk-tale is replaced by a metaphor which conveys the character's psychological attributes and relates directly to the sexual conflict. Once more, therefore, a traditional element of the folk-tale is not foresaken, but adapted, evolving into a fundamental element of Gogol's mature narrative art.

These examples will suffice to justify the contention that the tales of *Evenings* were the crucible in which Gogol forged the basic elements of his art and to illustrate the progression that characterises its development — a progression in which, as the American scholar James M. Holquist has written, "the conventions of the *Kunstmärchen*, fantasy by the book, according to rules, become gradually transformed by Gogol into a grammar of devices tailored to the demands of his own vision".[41] The inclusion of "Shpon'ka" in *Evenings*, we may assume, was designed precisely to highlight this evolutionary process which ultimately gave birth to the more famous stories that we will now examine.

FOOTNOTES TO CHAPTER II

1. This title is abbreviated hereafter to "Shpon'ka".
2. Setchkarev, p. 113.
3. Erlich, p. 45. Cf. Gippius, p. 39.
4. Driessen, p. 110.
5. References to "Shpon'ka" and the other tales of *Evenings* are all to volume 1 of *PSS* and are accordingly entered in the text by page number only in the remainder of this chapter.
6. Cf. the famous description in *Dead Souls* of nature's creation of Sobakevich (VI, 94-5).
7. See *GDS*, p. 12.
8. See ibid. pp. 15-16.
9. Quoted from B. M. Eykhenbaum, *"Skvoz' literaturu"*. *Sbornik statej* (Leningrad, 1924), p. 176.
10. See *GDS*, pp. 23-4.
11. See ibid., pp. 71-2.
12. See ibid. pp. 72-4.
13. The image of the spider was later to be more directly evoked in Gogol's portrait of Korobochka (see ibid. pp. 83-4, 86, 98).
14. See the reference to the fortune-telling book that Shpon'ka reads while in the army (288).
15. See *GDS*, pp. 87-9.
16. Cf. the remark that when Storchenko addresses his footman, "his voice imperceptibly became more and more menacing" (290).
17. See the narrator's terse description of him as "a fat man in a green frock-coat" (289).
18. Cf. his earlier admonition of his manservant in the inn for failing to "heat" (*razogret'*) the "hen" (*kuritsu*) that is served to him (290).
19. See *GDS*, pp. 97-8.
20. Cf. the "digression" in chapter 3 of *Dead Souls* which alludes to the conversion of Korobochka's husband from a Prometheus to a fly and grain of sand (VI, 49-50). See *GDS*, pp. 72-4.
21. See infra, pp. 90-1.
22. See *GDS*, pp. 80-1.
23. In general, the motif of sleep plays an important part in the tale in conveying Shpon'ka's lack of masculine vitality. Thus even during his army career, the narrator discloses, he was given to "lying on his bed" (286), and perhaps another variation of the motif, designed to convey his passivity on his first meeting with Storchenko, may be perceived in the reference to the pleasure that he derives from kissing the latter's "large cheeks" which "felt to his lips like soft pillows" (290).
24. See *PSS*, VI, 97, and *GDS*, p. 20.

25. See Setchkarev, p. 114.

26. Ibid.

27. Belyy, p. 103.

28. In reference to the general significance of ornithological imagery in Gogol's fiction, see *GDS*, pp. 31, 95-6. The relation of the image of the quail to his ornithological symbolism and the significance in his works of "ornithological sex" are also illustrated in the opening paragraph of chapter 5 of *Dead Souls*, in which the heart of Chichikov is compared to "a female quail (*perepyolka*) in a cage" (VI, 89) (see *GDS*, p. 31).

29. See ibid., pp. 77-8. 95-6.

30. See the editor's remark that "you can meet him in the market, where he is to be seen every morning before nine o'clock" (294).

31. See *GDS*, p. 44.

32. See his remark after eulogizing his wife's pies: "They can do anything, these women!" (107).

33. Italics mine.

34. The name Chichikov, derived from the verb *chikhat'* ("to sneeze"), is merely one of the numerous allusions in *Dead Souls* to the potency of the hero's nose.

35. Cf. the sentiment of the inveterate warrior and hunter Taras Bul'ba in *Mirgorod*: "A Cossack is not made to spend his life with women (*vozit'sya s babami*)" (II, 43).

36. See *GDS*, p. 105.

37. See infra, pp. 90-1.

38. Erlich, p. 30.

39. Cf. the rumour in "Christmas Eve" that the witch Solokha "cried out like a cock" (212).

40. See *GDS*, pp. 77-8.

41. James M. Holquist, "The Devil in Mufti: the *Märchenwelt* in Gogol's Short Stories", *PMLA*, 1967, No. 4, p. 353.

III

"OLD-WORLD LANDOWNERS"

Probably begun towards the end of 1832 and completed in 1833, "Old-World Landowners", the first of the four works in Gogol's second volume *Mirgorod*,[1] has been described as "one of the most perfect short stories in the whole of world literature".[2] Yet from the time of its first appearance, like most of Gogol's works, it has had a highly disconcerting effect on critics. Ostensibly, the narrator's purpose in the story is to acquaint the reader with a latter-day Philemon and Baucis, to prevail on us to share his pleasure as he seeks a respite from the hurly-burly of life in memories of the mutual devotion and enviable contentment enjoyed in the bosom of nature by the aged Ukrainian landowner Afanasy Ivanovich Tovstogub and his wife Pul'kheriya Ivanovna; and although the product of his efforts is a picture, in Belinsky's words, of "two parodies of mankind" living an "ugly, ludicrous, animal life",[3] it paradoxically contrives in the end to make a profound emotional impact, leaving us to ponder whether his tribute to the protagonists and their mode of existence is meant, after all, to be taken seriously or whether, despite his success in engaging our emotions, it masks a sustained indictment.

Belinsky's comments on the story vividly convey the usual reaction to it. He writes:

> Two parodies of mankind spend several decades drinking and eating, eating and drinking, and then, as is the age-old custom, they die. What, then, is the source of this charm? You see all the vulgarity and vileness of this ugly, ludicrous, animal life, yet at the same time you feel such a profound concern for the characters of the tale. You laugh at them, but without rancour, and then you sob with Philemon for his Baucis, sympathise with his deep, unearthly sorrow and vent your wrath on the worthless heir who squanders the two simpletons' property . . . Why is this?[4]

The same question, prompted by the difficulty of reconciling the characters' mode of existence with the narrator's eulogistic and compassionate attitude to them, has since been repeated in virtually every critical response to the story, and Belinsky offered the following answer:

> Because it is all very simple and therefore very true, because the author has found poetry even in this vulgar and ridiculous life; he has found the human feeling which propels and enlivens his characters: this feeling is habit.[5]

The first part of this answer has won little support, for in general critics have understandably been disinclined either to equate simplicity with truth or to include simplicity among Gogol's virtues, but the contention that the story moves the reader because he succeeds in extracting "poetry" from a relationship based on the "feeling" of habit has often been reiterated.[6] At the same time it is noticeable that the critics who have taken this view have usually felt obliged to couple the term "habit" with alleged synonyms, i.e. to offer their own interpretations of what "habit" in this context means. Concluding, for example, that it means "faithfulness", Driessen unequivocally affirms that Gogol is intent on idealising the "feeling",[7] and essentially the same view is expressed by Chizhevsky, who substitutes "calm and unobtrusive love", arguing that it "is contrasted with romantic love, this being passionate — and ... fickle".[8] In both cases, therefore, a "feeling" that would normally emerge in an unfavourable light when contrasted with love is converted by "synonyms" into an equally worthy object of idealisation. Very different, however, was the reaction of Shevyryov, who offered no euphemistic synonyms and, taking the narrator's praise of the two protagonists at its face value, felt that it was precisely "the ghastly thought of habit" that destroys the general harmony of the work.[9] Thus the "feeling" which forms the very basis of the central relationship in the story has evoked diametrically contrasting responses.

The question that has prompted these differences — how is the term "habit" to be interpreted here? — is certainly one of the major questions posed by the work, for the answer that we give to it will determine our attitude to the fundamental contrast in the tale between the world of the protagonists and the outside world. And unless we choose to straddle the fence, like Erlich who describes the tale as "a satiric idyll or a seedy pastoral ... neither a pure idyll nor a straight satire",[10] three options would seem to be open to us. We can subscribe to the view of Chizhevsky and Driessen that habit here is a noble "feeling" and that the world of the protagonists is therefore the positive pole of the contrast; we can also accept the latter judgment while taking the view of Shevyryov that the references to habit are a *faux pas* on Gogol's part which unnecessarily clouds the issue; and, finally, we can concur with Shevyryov's interpretation of habit as a negative or "ghastly" phenomenon and reach the different conclusion that the positive pole of the contrast is the outside world. Criticism has thus far inclined towards one of the first two options and, indeed, has yet to consider the third option seriously. The reason is quite simple: it presupposes the rejection of a view which hitherto has scarcely been questioned — namely, that the attitudes of the narrator (above all, his favourable disposition towards the protagonists) are basically those of Gogol himself. Thus Gippius, as if unaware of the question that he is begging, informs us that "Gogol, of course, does not conceal his sympathy for the old people",[11] and Karlinsky, asserting that Gogol "loves them, admires them and is charmed by them", has no hesitation in interpreting the narrator's uncomplimentary references to the

Ukrainians who "inundate" St. Petersburg (15) as a reflection of the author's personal antipathy to the "Ukrainian *nouveaux riches*".[12] Clearly the third option must be dismissed if, as these comments imply, narrator and author are one and the same. But in the following pages this view will be challenged. It will be argued that the narrator's eulogy is merely a facade concealing the author's critique and that the third option is accordingly the correct one, and it is perhaps in this connection that we should consider a modification that Gogol made after *Mirgorod* was first published in 1835.

It has already been noted that in this first edition Gogol gave the volume the subtitle "Tales Serving as a Continuation of *Evenings on a Farm near Dikan'ka*".[13] Why, we must ask, did he later withdraw it? In order to answer this question, we must first ask why he initially included it, and given the obvious differences of setting, period and style between the four works in the collection, only one answer would seem to be possible: that the subtitle was intended to indicate an underlying *thematic* connection between the two volumes. If, therefore, such a connection does exist — and it is hoped that our reading of "Old-World Landowners" will confirm that it does — why was the subtitle not retained? The major reason, it is suggested, was the change that Gogol had effected in *Mirgorod* in the function of the narrator. In *Evenings*, as we have seen, Gogol developed the technique of constructing a narrative on two levels, one of which is readily comprehensible, rich in comedy and absurdities and generally inoffensive, while the other is concealed, serious and polemical. The essential point, however, is that second level (the symbolic level), like the first, belongs to the editor and the narrators who are intent on concealing their primary objective from their female readers. The presence of the author himself, in consequence, is never in evidence. In *Mirgorod* the situation is quite different, for here Gogol exploits this technique of setting literal and symbolic levels of meaning in opposition to one another by identifying them with two conflicting points of view, i.e. by expressing himself on the symbolic level attitudes to the characters and events which differ notably from those expressed by the narrator. In this sense the stories of *Mirgorod* mark a significant transition in the development of Gogol's art, for the same kind of distinction between narrative levels expressive of conflicting attitudes was henceforth to characterise almost all his works, providing the major explanation, it is held, for his repeated adherence to the practice of interposing narrators between himself and the reader.

It is also conceivable that this important change in the function of the two-level narrative explains another puzzling feature of *Mirgorod* — namely, its two curious epigraphs: (1) "Mirgorod is a small town on the river Khorol. It has one rope factory, one brick-yard, four water-mills and forty-five windmills. (Zyablovsky's *Geography*);" and (2) "Although the bread rings (*bubliki*) are baked from black dough in Mirgorod, they are quite tasty. (From a traveller's diary)" (7). The combination here of a starkly factual statement with a statement containing one of Gogol's most important symbolic images (the image of heat) clothed in one of its commonest symbolic disguises (the verb "to bake") suggests that the purpose of the epigraphs may well be to emphasize from the start the coexistence of two distinct levels of meaning. But however that may be, it remains the fundamental contention of this chapter that the problems of interpretation posed by "Old-World Landowners", as by the other works in *Mirgorod*, can be satisfactorily resolved only if the existence of the two levels is recognized, and it is in the light of this claim that the story will be examined. Let us, then, turn our attention, in the first instance, to the relationship between the two main characters, which Karlinsky has described as "the only true and meaningful marriage that we find anywhere in Gogol".[14]

Certainly one of the first things that strike the reader is that the relationship is rather more complex than the narrator's account of it would seem to suggest. Although he assures us that "one could not look without sympathy at their mutual love" (15), evidence of a certain tension is not difficult to perceive. Not only is the marriage childless, but the protagonists are given to addressing one another with a formality which at least arouses our suspicions. Moreover, the phrase "mutual love" (*vzaimnaya lyubov'*) is replaced immediately afterwards in the description of the relationship by the term "attachment" (*privyazannost'*), a term which the narrator, evidently forgetting this earlier juxtaposition, clearly differentiates from "love" towards the end of the tale in his comment on Pul'kheriya Ivanovna's feelings for her cat: "It cannot be said that Pul'kheriya Ivanova felt any great love (*slishkom lyubila*) for it; she was simply attached (*privyazalas'*) to it, having become accustomed to always seeing it about" (28). We may deduce, therefore, that the statement similarly defines the true nature of her feelings for her husband.

The term "attachment", however, in this context has unexpected implications which become clear only in the light of the symbolic level of meaning imparted to certain details. Especially revealing in this connection is the tendency of Afanasy Ivanovich to lapse into the curious forms of provocation which are passed off by the narrator as simply playful teasing. It is noticeable, for example, that he derives a particular pleasure from playing on Pul'kheriya Ivanovna's evidently profound fear of fire. Thus two pages after inviting an abrupt riposte by complaining that his porridge is burnt (22), he subjects her to an exhausting interrogation in which verbs meaning "to burn" are repeated as many as seven times as he strives "playfully" to determine what she would do if the house were to burn down. Losing her self-control, she is finally impelled to exclaim: "God knows what you are saying! I don't want to listen to you! It's a sin to say it, and God punishes people for saying such things!" (24). Our initial reaction to these episodes is to regard them as little more than entertaining digressions designed, perhaps, to strengthen our affection for this ingenuous couple,[15] but evidence forthcoming from Gogol's other works suggests the possibility of a markedly different and much more important function. The main source of this evidence is the portrait of another Gogolian female who fears fire — once more that of

Korobochka in *Dead Souls*, in which the image of fire is employed as a recurrent symbol of the free human spirit.[16] Here we need to recall again the well-known "digression" in the context of Korobochka's portrait which has already been referred to in connection with the predicament of Storchenko and Masha's reply to Shpon'ka — the "digression" on the subject of modes of address, which concludes with the narrator's imaginative picture of a certain civil servant named Ivan Petrovich who is reduced from the status of Prometheus to that of a fly and a grain of sand (VI, 49-50). When it is disclosed in the course of Korobochka's ensuing dialogue with Chichikov that she shares a common patronymic with this luckless official (Nastas'ya Petrovna) and that her husband, a former Collegiate Secretary (and so also a civil servant) has been similarly reduced — in this case, like almost every other male on her estate, to a premature grave — we can scarcely doubt that Ivan Petrovich and Korobochka's husband are one and the same and that the narrator's flight of fantasy alludes directly to the latter's fate. As in the story of Afanasy Ivanovich and Pul'kheriya Ivanovna, Gogol links husband and wife by means of a common patronymic, and constructing his narrative on the basis of the allegorical theme of a woman's usurpation of the dominant masculine role, he obliquely compares the enslavement and ultimately extinction of the husband's spirit to the fall of Prometheus, the giver of fire to mankind and universal symbol of courageous defiance. It is precisely this disguised comparison that enables us to comprehend the implications of Korobochka's arresting description of the death of her blacksmith, who was the victim, she claims, of a fire that started inside him and emitted "a blue flame" on expiring (VI, 51). The conclusion suggested by these details is that fire is dreaded by Korobochka less as a destroyer of her material possessions than as a symbol of the free, Promethean human spirit which struggles to elude her masculine control, and there are strong grounds for believing that Pul'kheriya Ivanovna's fear of fire is similarly motivated.

The enslavement of Ivan Petrovich by Nastas'ya Petrovna, which is so subtly implied by the indicated "digression", is directly prefigured by Pul'kheriya Ivanovna's much more explicitly conveyed control over Afanasy Ivanovich, and we may perhaps assume that the common patronymic was meant in both cases to indicate that the marital relationship has been replaced by a fraternal relationship in which the "brother" is reduced by the "sister" to a state of helpless, childlike dependence. The dominant position of Pul'kheriya Ivanovna is immediately self-evident, for the narrator makes it quite clear that, like Vasilisa Kashporovna in "Shpon'ka" and Agafiya Fedoseyevna in "The Two Ivans", she readily undertakes "the entire burden of management" (19),[17] and the parent-child relationship is clearly reflected in the exchange that he quotes as an illustration of their formal manner of addressing one another: " 'Was it you who broke the chair, Afanasy Ivanovich?' 'Never mind, don't be angry, Pul'kheriya Ivanovna, it was I' " (15). Moreover, we may perhaps infer from the narrator's disclosure that the only bachelor in the house is the houseboy (19) that the position of Afanasy Ivanovich is paralleled by that of the male house-serfs, i.e. that every male in the house is similarly subject to female control quite apart from the overall control of Pul'kheriya Ivanova, for in an earlier version of the tale the female house-serfs are significantly endowed with the awesome physical dimensions of Shpon'ka's aunt (467). The impression conveyed, therefore, is that of a community which, by contrast with the communities of pastoral tradition,[18] is emphatically matriarchal.

At the same time the obvious relish with which Afanasy Ivanovich raises the bogy of fire can only be interpreted, if our assumptions are correct, as an indication that his spirit has not yet succumbed completely, i.e. that he has not yet sunk to the level of Ivan Petrovich, and a number of additional details were evidently included to reaffirm this point. Particularly noteworthy, for example, is his seemingly ludicrous aspiration to "go to war" which predictably elicits from Pul'kheriya Ivanovna the same kind of reaction as his references to fire. The way is prepared for his announcements on this subject by the revelation that he had once served in the army (15-16), a revelation that underlines his affinity not only with Shpon'ka but also with Manilov in *Dead Souls*. Each of these male characters undergoes the same experience — transformation from a "warrior" into a totally passive, ineffectual landowner — and in each case Gogol provides grounds for only one deduction: that the transformation is the result of a woman's influence.[19] And again the implications of this metamorphosis are suggested by the specifically sexual (i.e. masculine) associations of the "military motif" as most clearly disclosed by the portrait of Nozdryov, who not only contrives, as noted above, to rid himself of his wife soon after their marriage, but counts military men among his boon-companions, collects daggers and guns, boasts a hurdy-gurdy that pipes martial tunes, and finally becomes a "lieu-tenant" in the Homeric simile that describes his assault on Chichikov.[20] In the portrait of Nozdryov, as we have seen, the "military" cast of mind is inseparably associated with anti-feminism. It becomes an emblem of the masculine person-ality. The tendency, therefore, of Gogol's later heroes to follow Shpon'ka into retirement from the army[21] is a significant indicator of their psychological condition.

After listening attentively to the remarks of a guest about the imminence of war between Russia and France, Afanasy Ivanovich, we read, "pretending not to look at Pul'kheriya Ivanova", exclaims: "I am thinking of going to the war myself. Why on earth can't I go to the war?" (25). Turning to the guest, Pul'kheriya Ivanovna provides the answer:

How could an old man like him go to the war? The first soldier would shoot him! Yes, indeed he would! He'd simply take aim and shoot him .... How could he go to the war? His pistols have been rusty for years and are lying in the cupboard. You should just see them: why, gunpowder would burst their barrels before they'd fire a shot. He'd blow off his hands and disfigure his face and be wretched for the rest of his days (26).

Afanasy Ivanovich counters at once by threatening to buy new weapons, thereby prompting Pul'kheriya Ivanovna to launch into another vexatious outburst, but the dialogue ends abruptly at this point. Repeating almost verbatim his concluding comment on the dialogue about fire, the narrator adds: "Afanasy Ivanovich, pleased at having frightened Pul'kheriya Ivanovna a little, laughed as he sat bent up in his chair" (26). The threat turns out, therefore, to be a damp squib, nothing more than another example of playful teasing, and may thus be regarded, like the rusty condition of his pistols,[22] as simply additional testimony to Pul'kheriya Ivanovna's triumph.

The episode confirms that while the masculine (or "Nozdryovian") spirit and vitality of Afanasy Ivanovich are still alive, the sole evidence of their survival, if we exclude his laughter and the lingering smile on his face which the narrator contrasts with his wife's invariable gravity (15), is verbal. "You are simply fond of talking and nothing else," Pul'kheriya Ivanovna aptly remarks to him on one occasion (28). Like Manilov, he has lost completely the ability to translate word into action. Although we are told that, like the master of Manilovka, he "took very little interest in farming" (19), we learn two pages later that in his conversations with the farm labourers he displayed "an extraordinary knowledge of farming", yet the running of the estate, as we have observed, is undertaken solely by Pul'kheriya Ivanovna. The portrait of Afanasy Ivanovich hinges entirely on this discrepancy between thought and deed, between a mind that still reveals glimpses of independence and vitality and an impotent, emasculated body that has become solely a receptacle for his wife's concoctions — concoctions which perhaps not coincidentally, like the repast with which Chichikov is served by Korobochka, are conspicuously lacking in the "masculine" nourishment of meat.[23] The portrait reflects the terminal stage in the emasculation of the "fine young fellow" (*molodets*) who at the age of thirty, at which he married, was a captain in the army, possessed a sporty "embroidered waistcoat" and was even capable of effecting a dashing elopement (16). As the narrator puts it with significant emphasis, "that was a very long time ago, that was all over, and Afanasy Ivanovich hardly ever recalled it" (15-16). Now, like Pul'kheriya Ivanovna's cart-horses which had also, we are informed, once served in the army (20), he has been reduced to the living death of total subservience. Ironically, the wife who responds to his fantasies about fire by threatening him with the punishment of God and insists that his pistols would disfigure his face inflicts a far more radical disfigurement of his masculine spirit, transforming him from a "fine young fellow" into a pathetic child.

The affinity between Pul'kheriya Ivanovna and Korobochka, which parallels the affinity between Afanasy Ivanovich and the deceased Ivan Petrovich, is strengthened by many other common details in their portraits and in the descriptions of the domains over which they preside. In Pul'kheriya Ivanovna's portrait, for example, we encounter once more the familiar "Korobochkan" motif of deafening noise. Especially noteworthy are the common details in the descriptions of their carriages. Just as the entry of Korobochka into the town of N. at the end of chapter 8 of *Dead Souls* is heralded by "the noise and creaking of iron clamps and rusty screws" which "woke up a policeman at the other end of the town" (VI, 176), so Pul'kheriya Ivanovna's departure on a tour of inspection of her forests is signalled by "strange sounds" which "filled the air". "Every nail and iron clamp," we read, "clanked so loudly that even at the mills it could be heard that the mistress was driving out of the yard, though the distance was fully a mile and a half" (20). Likewise the cacophony of "singing" doors in Pul'kheriya Ivanovna's "little house" (17-18) is described, like Shpon'-ka's welcoming party, in terms which immediately recall the description of the canine choir that announces Chichikov's entry into Korobochka's courtyard (VI, 42). Still more striking, however, is the evidence of Pul'kheriya Ivanovna's susceptibility to the significant idiosyncrasy reflected in Korobochka's name — the idiosyncrasy which, as we have suggested earlier, is conveyed by the syntactic structure of the description of Vasilisa Kashporovna's dogs: namely, an obsessive preoccupation with various types of container. She too is possessed of a pathological urge to thrust things into boxes, chests, bags and sacks. Thus we read: "Pul'kheriya Ivanovna's room was filled with chests and boxes, large and small.[24] Numerous little bags and sacks of flower seeds, vegetable seeds and melon seeds hung on the walls" (17).[25] And the contents of her larder, we are told, are carried out "in wooden boxes, sieves, trays and other receptacles for holding fruit" (22).

In both portraits the motif of "containers" obviously alludes to a passion for hoarding, to a grotesquely inflated acquisitive instinct, but it also seems to possess the additional implications that have already been noted — implications which relate directly to the common allegorical theme. At a more profound level the images which comprise the motif function as symbolic analogues epitomizing the essential character of the domains which the two hoarders administer, for both domains, like that of Vasilisa Kashporovna, are indeed "boxes" in a very real sense, "boxes" skilfully designed by their creators for the purpose of stifling the human spirit. While the realm of Korobochka is sealed by the sturdy fences with which Chichikov's carriage collides on his arrival and is neatly divided up, like Chichikov's box, into little pens and compartments, the estate of Pul'-kheriya Ivanova is so effectively insulated by its palisade, we are told, that "not a single desire flits beyond it" (13). And the same concern with insulation is also apparent in the extreme seclusion of the two "boxes". The estate of Koroboch-ka, it will be recalled, is discovered by Chichikov only by accident and after a painful nocturnal journey across ploughed fields (VI, 41-3), and only with the aid of a guide does he re-establish contact with the outside world. The comparable seclusion of Pul'kheriya Ivanovna's realm is obliquely conveyed by the title of the story, which adds a temporal dimension to its spatial seclusion, and is explicitly indicated by the narrator's opening words: "I am very fond of the modest life of those solitary owners of remote villages", a life which he describes a few lines later as "that extraordinarily secluded life" (13). Although the two ladies are pictured setting forth in their clanking carriages, it is made quite clear that only in exceptional circumstances are they given to emerging from behind their fences. Only her suspicions of her steward, it seems, impel Pul'kheriya Ivanovna to inspect her forests, and the event is never repeated (20).[26]

Another conspicuous feature of Pul'kheriya Ivanovna's "box" is its "lowness". The adjective "low" recurs in the narrator's description with intriguing persistence, and he uses it invariably in diminutive form (*nizen'kiy*). "I can see now," he writes, "the low little house (*nizen'kiy domik*)" (13), and the same epithet is later applied both to its diminutive rooms (16) and even to the grass and fruit trees in the garden (13-14). Superficially, of course, the diminutives are hypocoristic forms expressive of the narrator's affection and nostalgia for this secluded world, but again it is possible to detect the familiar ironic tension between superficial and symbolic meanings. Their less obvious function is to reinforce the idea of oppressive constriction which is implicit in the meaning of the epithet, to explain, in effect, why the "humble (literally "low" (*nizmennuyu*)) bucolic life", which the narrator praises at the end of the long introductory paragraph of the story, induces the state of mind, as he puts it, in which "one involuntarily renounces all audacious dreams" (14). Reminding us of the various "boxes" in which Khoma Brut is confined in "Viy" — a sheep-pen, an inn and the house of the *sotnik*, to all of which the epithet *nizen'kiy* is similarly applied (185, 191, 194) — the diminutives allude, in short, to the fundamental character of the "box" in which Afanasy Ivanovich is involuntarily emasculated.

It is in relation to this symbolic role of the motif of "lowness" that we need to consider the function in the tale of the familiar motif of heat, which is used here by Gogol to capture one of his most telling ironic effects. The irony is perceptible in the following comment on the protagonists' bedroom:

> The room in which Afanasy Ivanovich and Pul'kheriya Ivanovna slept was so hot that few people would be capable of remaining a few hours in it. But Afanasy Ivanovich, to add to matters, used to sleep on the stove-bench in order to be warmer, though the intense heat often made him get up a few times in the night and walk about the room (23).

Here, of course, Afanasy Ivanovich's craving for heat may be related to his fascination with fire. In other words, his desire for a more intense heat conveys his craving for restoration of the "fire" that he has lost. But his periodic retreats from the source of the heat are a vivid indication that he seeks from it the opposite of what it has to give, thus implying that the apparent connection between the motifs of heat and fire is entirely illusory; and indeed, it soon becomes evident that far from signifying the attributes that he has lost, the heat is ironically a symbol of his enslavement. The passage, in effect, is a graphic representation of the "steaming", "stewing" and "desiccation" of Afanasy Ivanovich's soul in the "low", oppressive pressure-cooker of Pul'kheriya Ivanovna's "little house" and accordingly explains why Pul'kheriya Ivanovna, like Vasilisa Kashporovna and Storchenko's mother, is cast in the "infernal" role of indefatigable cook. Her housekeeping, we read, "consisted of continually locking up and unlocking the larder and of pickling, drying and boiling countless masses of fruit and vegetables" (19). It is true that, unlike Agafiya Fedoseyevna in "The Two Ivans", she is not attributed with the habit of actually rubbing down her male charge with vinegar,[27] but there can be little doubt that her devotion to pickling, drying and stewing fruit alludes to her similar assault on his yielding spirit. The stewing and desiccation of the fruit are metaphors of the emasculation of Afanasy Ivanovich, while the larder to which his eye is constantly drawn is a microcosm of the "hot-house" in which this process is effected. Ironically, the pickled vegetables that Pul'kheriya Ivanovna recommends as cures for bodily afflictions and pours incessantly down her husband's throat are symbols of the condition to which his soul is being reduced[28] and, as such, they expose the irony both of the allusion to Ovid's myth and of the narrator's praise for the "bucolic life". The metamorphosis of Philemon and Baucis into trees is replaced by the metamorphosis of Afanasy Ivanovich into a stewed, desiccated and pickled vegetable.[29]

Recalling, therefore, the implications in "The Sorochintsy Fair" of Khivrya's seduction of the priest's son (who also, incidentally, bears the name Afanasy Ivanovich), we may now comprehend why Gogol inserts two religious allusions into the description of Pul'kheriya Ivanovna's culinary activities: the revelation that she was initiated in the art of pickling mushrooms with cloves by a "kind woman" who "professed the Turkish religion", and her disclosure that she learnt to boil pumpkins in vinegar from "Father Ivan" (27). In the figure of Father Ivan, another precursor of Korobochka's associate Father Kiril, the Orthodox Church, like everything else on the estate, is shown to be subordinate to Pul'kheriya Ivanovna's will and is accordingly attributed with the capacity of the infidel for corrupting souls. Hence the "confinement" of the picture of "some bishop" in the "box" of one of her "narrow frames" (*uzen'kikh ram*) (17). Here the diminutive *uzen'kiy* echoes the diminutive *nizen'kiy* and is likewise expressive of stifling constriction. The frames that enclose in the "little house" the pictures of the bishop, Peter III and the Duchesse de La Vallière (a mistress of Louis XIV) symbolise the triumph of Pul'kheriya Ivanovna over three inimical forces: the authority of the Church, the authority of her husband[30] and the tradition of female subservience.

At first sight, of course, it seems difficult to reconcile this sinister aspect of Pul'kheriya Ivanovna's activities with her affability and generosity in the presence of guests, but the contradiction is more apparent than real. Not for nothing is the impression conveyed that the guests who visit the "little house" are exclusively male, acquaintances of Afanasy Ivanovich who bring news of the outside world which momentarily reanimates his atrophied masculine instincts. And equally noteworthy is Pul'kheriya Ivanovna's reluctance to release them, her habit of threatening them with the spectre of brigands allegedly waiting for them beyond the barrier of her palisade. The narrator informs us that the hospitality and readiness to please of the hosts "were so gently expressed in their faces, were so in keeping with them, that one could not help falling in with their wishes" (24-5), but the details mentioned leave little doubt that the "wishes" of the wife are quite different from those of the husband. The hospitality of Afanasy Ivanovich, like that of Manilov in *Dead Souls,* is explained by the desire for restored contact with life which the guests represent for him, but that of Pul'kheriya Ivanovna is inspired by the prospect of more victims, by the opportunity to pickle more male souls and consign them to the boxes in her larder. It reflects the insatiable appetite for male souls that she shares with Korobochka. Employing once more as her most powerful bait, like Khivrya, the culinary delights which ironically symbolise the fate that she plans for them, she brings to bear on her husband's friends the potent charms to which her Christian name alludes, the charms which evidently proved irresistible to the young Afanasy Ivanovich. But now, it seems, their power has waned. Heedless of her warnings, the guests, though temporarily bewitched, eventually depart, leaving the enchantress to refocus her entire attention on her impotent, "leaden-eyed" (35) husband.

In addition, however, to Afanasy Ivanovich and the guests there is another male in the work who similarly feels the full force of Pul'kheriya Ivanovna's charms — the narrator. Hence his statement: "Pul'kheriya Ivanovna was most interesting to me when she was treating a guest to her snacks" (26). And it is precisely his experience of their impact which provides the answer to most of the major problems posed by the story — above all, the problem of the seemingly inappropriate tone in which the tale is related. For it is now clear that this tone and the angle of vision that it implies are intended to complement, as an explicit exposé, the oblique evidence of the power of the "beautiful" siren's lure that is furnished by the portrait of Afanasy Ivanovich. Like the former "warrior", the narrator is himself cast in the role of a victim of this lure and thus presents himself as a totally uncritical apologist both of Pul'kheriya Ivanovna and of her stifling "box". Identifying the narrator with the point of view of a seduced victim, Gogol is able to combine in the tale two diametrically contrasting attitudes to his heroine and her secluded realm — the apologist's eulogy which is wholly explicit and his own indictment conveyed by symbol — thus producing the remarkable "double-edged" quality that characterizes its language.

Maintaining literal and symbolic meanings in a state of perpetual contradiction, Gogol creates a code in which words denote the opposite of their ostensible referents. Thus while the "box" is represented as an oasis of good, the outside world with its violent passions is condemned as the realm of the devil. Indeed, every manifestation of life, of vitality, audacity, resourcefulness, violence (for example, the pilfering of the steward and elder and the disruptive impact of the "military" heir and the "staff captain in a faded uniform" (38) who assists him), excites the narrator's righteous indignation, while the domain in which a man is stripped of these attributes and reduced to the state of a pickled vegetable is projected as a haven of peace — or "Peaceville" (*Mirgorod*) — which is "so quiet, so quiet that for a moment one is lost in oblivion and imagines that those passions, desires and restless promptings of the evil spirit which trouble the world do not exist at all and that you have only beheld them in some dazzling dream" (13). The narrator continues:

> Even as my *britzka* was driving up to the steps of that little house, my soul passed into a remarkably pleasant and peaceful mood (*spokoynoye sostoyaniye*). The horses galloped merrily up to the steps; the coachman very calmly (*prespokoyno*) climbed down from the box . . .; even the barking set up by the phlegmatic Barboses, Brovkas and Zhuchkas was pleasant to my ears (14).

Here the coexistence of the two conflicting levels of meaning is immediately apparent in the accumulation of words ("quiet", "oblivion", "dream", "peaceful", "calmly", "phlegmatic") which denote one thing for the narrator and something quite different for the author: at once an ideal existence and a living death.

Especially noteworthy is the reference to the dogs, which present a very different spectacle from the canine symbols of Vasilisa Kashporovna's personality or the yelping, flesh-eating hunting hounds which complement the "military motif" as symbols of the "Nozdryovian" attributes in chapter 4 of *Dead Souls*. Like the coachmen and lackeys on the estate (21), they are "phlegmatic" and bear names which allude directly to their fate. The significance of their names — at least of the name "Brovka" — is revealed by the story of the Cossack Spirid in "Viy" about the huntsman Mikita, who allegedly "knew every dog as well as his own father". We read further:

> He'd whistle: "Here, Brigand! Here, Swifty!", and he'd gallop off on his horse at full speed; and it was impossible to say which would outrace the other, he the dog, or the dog him . . . But not long ago he began to stare incessantly at the young mistress. Whether he had actually fallen in love with her or whether she had bewitched him, anyway the man was done for, he became completely effeminate (*obabilsya*) . . . As soon as the mistress looks at him, he drops the bridle out of his hand, calls Brigand Brovka, becomes flustered and doesn't know what he's doing (202-3).

Again we see here clear evidence of the close relationship between the "hunting", "military" and "canine" motifs. Like the "warrior" Afanasy Ivanovich, the huntsman Mikita is emasculated by a woman, and the symbol of his emasculation is his replacement of the name "Brigand" by "Brovka", which alludes to the suppression of his own masculine, canine instincts.[31] In the light of this parallel we can appreciate the force of Afanasy Ivanovich's comments on his wife's cat: "I don't know, Pul'kheriya Ivanovna, what you find in the cat. What use is she? If you had a dog, then it would be a different matter: one can take a dog hunting, but what use is a cat?" (28). Immediately the narrator seeks to assure us that "it made no difference to Afanasy Ivanovich whether it was a cat or a dog" (28), but the "canine" symbol contradicts his remark. Conveying Afanasy Ivanovich's nostalgia for the masculine activity of hunting, which is the passion of Nozdryov and Shpon'ka's aunt, and implying the inadequacy for this purpose of "phlegmatic Barboses, Brovkas and Zhuchkas", the hero's comments provide additional evidence that his emasculation is not yet complete, and they accordingly provoke another heated response from Pul'kheriya Ivanovna:

> Oh, be quiet, Afanasy Ivanovich. You are fond of talking and nothing else. A dog is dirty, a dog makes a mess, a dog breaks everything,[32] while a cat is a quiet creature; she does no harm to anyone (28).

Thus the quality prized in the cat is the quality prized by the narrator in Pul'kheriya Ivanovna's entire domain — its "quietness" — and his unqualified approval of this quietness is a conclusive indication that he has succumbed even more fully to Pul'kheriya Ivanovna's spell than her hapless spouse. The barking of "phlegmatic Brovkas" may be pleasant to the narrator's ears, but the ear of Afanasy Ivanovich is cocked for the bark of a Brigand, for the sounds of life beyond the palisade where, according to Pul'kheriya Ivanovna, brigands lie in wait.

The image of the cat, of course, offers additional testimony to Pul'kheriya Ivanovna's kinship with the long line of witches in *Evenings*, and its presence serves to confirm that we are as entitled to use the term "bewitchment" to characterize her power over her subjects as is Spirid in his description of the "mistress's" power over Mikita. Clearly more important, however, than the cat itself are the implications of its disappearance — an event which appears to be weakly motivated but which may now be seen to be, in reality, the culmination of the entire sequence of events in the preceding development of the work which has attracted our particular attention: namely, of the sporadic confrontations between the protagonists which are attributed to Afanasy Ivanovich's weakness for teasing and of the various other episodes and details which similarly testify to the competing lure of the outside world, for example, Pul'kheriya Ivanovna's inability to prevent her female house-serfs from becoming pregnant, despite clothing them in "striped petticoats" (18) which, like Korobochka's "striped wallpaper" (VI, 45), suggest the notion of bars and may be seen as an extension of the image of the palisade.[33] The cat is driven to breach the palisade by the same urge that impels Afanasy Ivanovich to question his guests so intensively about their experiences and current affairs,[34] by the same craving for restored contact with life in the raw, with creatures of flesh and blood for whom life is an endless succession of ups and downs which may bring hardship and deprivation, but which also bring excitement, emotion, passion. The life to which Afanasy Ivanovich's thoughts are still drawn is this essentially animal life to which his surname Tovstogub ("thick lips") conceivably alludes and which is the antithesis of his "bucolic", or vegetal, existence in the "box". It is his own pre-marital existence, the existence denoted by the "military motif" and celebrated in the battle scenes of "Taras Bul'ba", and it is plainly its emphatically animal character that explains the choice of an animal — moreover, a female animal — to illustrate the force of its lure. The triumph of "Nozdryovian" masculinity in the animal kingdom contrasts with the tragicomedy of emasculation in the human realm. And not surprisingly, of course, the cat's surrender earns it a sharp reproof from the narrator (30), while her feline tempters in the forest, whose skill as thieves (or disruptive invaders of the "box"[35]) links them with the steward and elder, are scornfully but most aptly compared to "a detachment of soldiers enticing a silly peasant girl" (29).

What interpretation, therefore, can we place on the causal connection that seems to exist between the cat's disappearance and its mistress's death — a death that takes place, in the words of one commentator, "for no apparent reason at all"[36]? In the light of our observations the answer does not seem too elusive. In his first reference to the cat the narrator mentions that it "almost always lay curled up at her feet" (28), thus evoking, as one critic has indicated, the image of a child[37] which is similarly used, as we have seen, to characterize the position of Afanasy Ivanovich. The latter's contemptuous remarks about it, however, and his call for a dog suggest a much greater degree of subservience, and since the cat is the cat of a witch, this seems entirely fitting. And yet it is precisely this most dependent of the mistress's subjects that chooses to leave her. Far exceeding in importance the other indications of her inability to insulate her realm, the defection of the cat represents for Pul'kheriya Ivanovna the most conclusive evidence of her ebbing powers and, as such, is a presentiment of death and prefigures the collapse of her "box".[38] And here we might note the suggestive parallel between the flight of the cat from the box-like estate and the flight of the witch's breath from the "box" of her body. The phrase *dykhaniye yeyo uletelo* (literally "her breath flew away") (32) may be related, like the image of the dead quail in "Shpon'ka" and the birds that fall to Vasilisa Kashporovna's gun, to the diverse ornithological symbols of freedom which form an integral part of Gogol's fictional universe[39] and, more directly, to the narrator's reference to the singing of the larks in his description of the funeral. Here the air is filled with the singing not of restrictive doors but of birds and with the cries of children who, unlike the invariably sleeping houseboy, "raced and skipped along the road" (33).[40]

But despite the imminent collapse of the "box" and the loss of the more submissive of her two "children", Pul'kheriya Ivanovna does not lose the other. We have only to read the narrator's description of the widower to be convinced of her unqualified triumph, for it predictably transpires that the emasculation of the former "warrior" is no longer reversible. Even in the physical absence of his oppressor, the animal life remains beyond his reach; the ability to act has been irretrievably lost; and to the end he remains a helpless child who has even lost the ability to feed himself. And again we might note the canine parallel – the narrator's reference, in the description of his visit to the estate five years after the mistress's death, to the blindness and lameness of "those same Barboses and Brovkas" (34). Bequeathing to her husband her satin dress "with crimson stripes" for adaptation into a dressing-gown (30-1), Pul'kheriya Ivanovna retains her control over him even in death, and she has only to whisper his name from beyond the grave in the "deathly, horrible quietness" of the garden to prompt his immediate compliance.

Despite the echo of the episode in Shpon'ka's dream in which the hero rushes into the garden only to be assailed by heat and by "wives" in his hat, pocket and ear (I, 307), the well-known passage in which the narrator "digresses" to recall experiences from his childhood similar to that of Afanasy Ivanovich in the garden has been interpreted by critics, like so many of Gogol's "digressions", as little more than an incidental authorial reminiscence.[41] The image of "deathly quietness", however, which clearly alludes to Pul'kheriya Ivanovna's presence and continuing control, is merely one indication of its direct relevance to the fiction. The essential feature of the passage is that the fundamental opposition in the tale between the viewpoints of narrator and author is combined with a second opposition between the viewpoints of the narrator as adult and child – an opposition that Gogol creates by reintroducing the idea of freedom from oppression which is earlier associated with the children at the funeral. Recalling his childhood reactions to such experiences, the narrator uses such adjectives as "deathly" and "horrible" to describe precisely the kind of "quietness" which in the present, as an adult and victim of the witch's charms, he values so highly. Again, in short, we perceive here the symbolic associations of age which are apparent not only in the reference to the children at the funeral but also in the contrast between the youth and old age of Afanasy Ivanovich[42] – associations which suggest an additional explanation of Gogol's choice of epithet in the title of the story and which enable us to appreciate the threat that is implicit in Pul'kheriya Ivanovna's remark to her steward, Nichipor, on witnessing the "thinning" of her forests: "Mind that the hair on your head does not grow as thin" (20). In effect, the resourceful Nichipor is being threatened here with the fate of Afanasy Ivanovich, with the fate of premature ageing inflicted by the punishment of having his forelock "tugged", like the miller of Shpon'ka's aunt, by his mistress's "masculine hand".[43] And finally, we might note the irony of the narrator's statement at the end of his "digression", for it alludes to the entire tragedy of Afanasy Ivanovich of which, in all appearance, he (the narrator) is totally unconscious: "I usually ran out of the garden in a great panic hardly able to breathe, and calmed down only when I met some person, the sight of whom dispelled the terrible spiritual loneliness" (37). Contrary to the narrator's intentions, the phrases "great panic" and "terrible spiritual loneliness" are essentially a retrospective definition of Afanasy Ivanovich's state of mind as he languishes in the "box", and it is precisely his inability to "run out" of it, contrasting with the success of the cat and of the peasants who take advantage of the heir's destructive measures (38), which constitute his tragic dilemma.

Towards the end of the story, therefore, the supernatural element is introduced to express the idea of a degree of enslavement which even death is powerless to affect. Just as the dead witch in "Viy" contrives the death of Khoma Brut, so Pul'kheriya Ivanovna, having controlled her husband in life, seeks to maintain her control by luring him after her into the realm of the dead, and his obedience to her whispered summons denotes the final extinction of his "flickering" spirit. Afanasy Ivanovich, we read, "submitted with the readiness of an obedient child", and with the words "Lay me beside Pul'kheriya Ivanovna" on his lips, he "melted like a candle and at last flickered out (*ugas*)" (37), thus revealing the irony of his Christian name which is derived from the Greek *athanasia* ("immortality"). The immortal human spirit turns out in Gogol's tale to be tragically mortal.[44]

With remarkable skill, therefore, Gogol sustains to the end the expressive interplay between contrasting levels of meaning which is the source of the tale's irony, creating perhaps the most deceptive narrative that ever issued from his deceptive pen. But for the purposes of the present enquiry the most important result of the analysis is the confirmation that it provides of the continuity of Gogol's allegorical theme and of the symbolic system that he had developed to express it. It is true, of course, that between Shpon'ka and his aunt and the two "old-world landowners" there are striking differences. Thus Pul'kheriya Ivanovna, like Korobochka, would seem to lack Vasilisa Kashporovna's formidable physique and displays no hint of enthusiasm for her outdoor pursuits. Yet it is clear that neither the absence of these symbolic elements from her portrait nor the changed appearance of others invalidates the argument that, like Shpon'ka and Afanasy Ivanovich, they are essentially variations of a single type. The only significant difference is that the more explicit indicators of Vasilisa Kashporovna's symbolic sexual characteristics have been discarded with the result that a portrait which contains many of the same symbolic elements creates superficially a quite different impression, prompting Karlinsky to describe its subject as "Gogol's most attractively presented, safest, and least threatening female character".[45] The transition, in short, from Shpon'ka's aunt to Pul'kheriya

Ivanovna is basically a transition to more oblique methods of portraiture and to a more refined, allusive and selective use of the symbolic system developed in *Evenings*, and it is precisely this transition that Gogol effects by creating with the aid of his distanced narrator the illusion of a paean to the female who is the object of the tale's indictment.

In respect of its position, therefore, in the sequence of Gogol's works, if not chronologically,[46] "Old-World Landowners" may justly be viewed as the first major example of his mature allegorical art. Never before, not even in "Shpon'-ka", had a symbolic relationship between the sexes formed the basis of such a complex, condensed and subtly ironic allegory in which almost every word seems to point in two directions simultaneously. It is as much these qualities of the allegory as its expressive ingredients which foreshadow his achievement in the best of the "Petersburg tales" and *Dead Souls.*

FOOTNOTES TO CHAPTER III

1. References to "Old-World Landowners" and the other works in *Mirgorod* are all to volume 2 of *PSS* and are entered in the text in this chapter by page number only.
2. Driessen, p. 115.
3. *N. V. Gogol' v russkoy kritike* (Moscow, 1953), p. 44.
4. Ibid., pp. 44-5.
5. Ibid., p. 45.
6. Cf., for example, Setchkarev's comment: "Gogol's art has here succeeded in elevating the lowest level of human existence to the level of a Platonic Idea" (Setchkarev, p. 137).
7. Driessen, p. 128.
8. D. Chizhevsky, "Neizvestnyy Gogol'", *Novyy zhurnal*, vol. 27, 1951, p. 134.
9. *N. V. Gogol' v russkoy kritike*, p. 65.
10. Erlich, p. 58.
11. Gippius, p. 83.
12. Karlinsky, pp. 62, 65.
13. Cf. his reference to *Mirgorod* in a letter to M. P. Pogodin of 31 January 1835 as "my continuation of *Evenings*" (X, 351).
14. Karlinsky, p. 63.
15. Cf. Driessen's comment: "We smile because it is love which expresses itself in that senseless playing with childlike anxiety" (Driessen, p. 123).
16. See *GDS*, pp. 72-4, 103-4.
17. See the reference to Agafiya Fedoseyevna: "She carried off the keys and took the whole house into her own hands." Ivan Nikiforovich, we read, "obeyed her like a child, and although he sometimes tried to argue with her, Agafiya Fedoseyevna always gained the upper hand" (240-1).
18. See R. Poggioli's observation: "The pastoral, whether it deals with material, or with emotional and spiritual happiness, is a typically masculine dreamworld" ("Gogol's 'Old-Fashioned Landowners': an Inverted Eclogue", *Indiana Slavic Studies*, vol. 3, 1963, p. 58).
19. For a discussion of the oblique communication of this point in the portrait of Manilov, see *GDS*, pp. 61-2.

20. See the numerous echoes of Nozdryov's portrait in the brief description at the end of "Old-World Landowners" of the former lieutenant who inherits the estate.

21. Other examples are Ivan Nikiforovich in "The Two Ivans" and Chertokutsky in "The Carriage".

22. Cf. the broken gun of Ivan Nikiforovich in "The Two Ivans" (234).

23. Cf., in contrast, the saddle of mutton with which Chichikov is regaled at the table of Sobakevich (VI, 98-100) and the "raw meat" on which Nozdryov feeds his wolf-cub (VI, 73).

24. Note the emphasis of the motif in the Russian: "sundukami, yashchikami, yashchichkami i sunduchkami."

25. The implicit irony of these references to seeds has been noted by Richard Peace in his essay "Gogol's *Old World Landowners*", *The Slavonic and East European Review*, vol. 53, 1975, p. 509.

26. Cf. the statement in "Shpon'ka" that Vasilisa Kashporovna "very rarely drove out" in her chaise (I, 304).

27. See the description of Ivan Nikiforovich's torment (212).

28. Cf. the irony of the narrator's comment on the demands made by Pul'kheriya Ivanovna on her guests' powers of consumption: "I wonder whether the very air of the Ukraine has not some particular property which helps digestion, for if anyone here were to take it into his head to eat in that way, he would undoubtedly find himself lying in his coffin instead of his bed" (27).

29. We may perhaps assume in this connection that Gogol had noted the evidence of Baucis's skill at pickling adduced by Ovid's reference to the "autumnal cherries preserved in pickle" ("Conditaque in liquida corna autumnalia faece") with which she feeds her divine visitors (*Metamorphoses*, VIII, 665).

30. The allusion, of course, is to the usurpation of Peter's throne by his wife, Catherine.

31. It may be noted that among the prototypes of Gogol's two "old-world landowners" suggested by contemporaries were an old married couple named Brovkov (see the reminiscences of S. A. Kapnist-Skalon in *Vospominaniya i rasskazy deyateley taynykh obshchestv 1820-kh godov* (Moscow, 1931), pp. 318-9).

32. See the allusion to the chair broken by Afanasy Ivanovich.

33. Perhaps the same idea is conveyed by the "woolen petticoats" of Vasilisa Kashporovna's female servants in "Shpon'ka" (I, 293).

34. See the narrator's statement: "He always listened with a pleasant smile to the guests who visited him; sometimes he talked himself, but more often he asked questions . . . As he questioned you, he showed great interest and curiosity about the circumstances of your life, your failures and successes" (16).

35. Cf. the sparrows and magpies which attack Korobochka's fruit trees (VI, 48).

36. N. M. Kolb-Seletski, "Gastronomy, Gogol, and His Fiction", *The Slavic Review*, vol. 29, 1970, p. 56.

37. See Poggioli, p. 64.

38. An ironic additional testimony to her decline is her attempt to win back the cat by feeding it on meat (29).

39. Cf. once more the ornithological foes of Korobochka.

40. The role of the children here as symbols of freedom is perhaps foreshadowed in "Shpon'ka" by Vasilisa Kashporovna's inability to control the children who remove the nails from the back of her chaise (I, 296).

41. See, for example, Mochul'sky, p. 136.

42. Cf. the narrator's question as he contemplates Afanasy Ivanovich during his last visit to the estate: "Are all our strong impulses, the whole whirlwind of our desires and boiling passions merely the result of our bright youth . . . ?" (36).

43. Pul'kheriya Ivanovna's threat may also be related to the fears of the sacristan in "Christmas Eve" that "his better half, whose terrible hand had already turned his thick braid into a very thin one, might learn of his doings" (I, 218), and to the protective action taken by Solopy Cherevik in "The Sorochintsy Fair" after a sharp exchange with Khivrya: "He instantly covered his head with his hands, doubtless expecting that his enraged spouse would lose no time in sinking her wifely claws into his hair" (I, 120).

44. The name Pul'kheriya, as we have seen, is equally expressive, but rather more striking is the irony of the name that Gogol initially gave his heroine: Nastasiya (459), which is derived from the Greek for "resurrection". As indicated above, this name (in the form "Nastas'ya") was later given to Korobochka.

45. Karlinsky, p. 63.

46. Although it is the first of the four works in *Mirgorod*, it seems to have been written after the last ("The Two Ivans"), though the date appended to the latter work when it was first published has been queried by scholars.

IV

"THE NOSE"

If "Old-World Landowners" is the most deceptive of Gogol's stories, "The Nose" is certainly the most perplexing. Naturally enough, there are still many readers who readily invoke Pushkin's description of the tale as "a joke" and argue fervently that any attempt to interpret its bizarre content as expressive of some single all-embracing idea is a totally misguided and futile exercise. But inevitably the work has continued to inspire such attempts. Not only does it seem improbable, as N. I. Oulianoff has observed,[1] that Gogol's state of mind was conducive to the writing of jokes in the "terrible year"[2] of 1833 when the first complete draft is assumed to have been written; it seems equally unlikely, had it been conceived as nothing more than a joke, that he would have expended so much time and effort on it in the years that followed. Moreover, the numerous echoes in the story of episodes and details in works of more obviously serious intent likewise reinforce the feeling that amusement was not his sole objective.

For a variety of reasons, however, the interpretations offered by critics have failed to banish scepticism. Predictably, they display the paradox that character- izes most interpretative studies of Gogol's works: their plausibility is inversely proportionate to their comprehensiveness. The interpretations which have been most favourably received are precisely those that are based on the most stringent selections of fictional material, while attempts to extract a coherent meaning from the *minutiae* have tended to be greeted with ridicule. Twenty-six years ago, for example, a seven-page analysis of the story by H. E. Bowman produced the persuasive conclusion, which has been reiterated more recently in Erlich's eight-page survey,[3] that it is basically a "grotesque laugh at the absurd impor- tance of appearances in a world of appearances",[4] and this, one suspects, is the view to which most readers would subscribe. It is significant, however, that in reaching his conclusion Bowman not only makes no reference to the content of more than half the story; perplexed by the apparent failure of chapter 1 and chapter 2 to "mesh", he also feels entitled to suggest that "this is a defect in Gogol's creation".[5] His superficially plausible conclusion, in short, rests on an implicit invitation to ignore large sections of the work and on explicit reserva- tions about its aesthetic merits.

A similar disregard for the more intractable ingredients of the tale is also perceptible in the more detailed studies of Gukovsky, who likewise interprets it as a social satire,[6] and Oulianoff, who attempts with considerable ingenuity to substantiate the argument that the nose is a symbol of the devil. Thus Oulianoff is not only at a loss to explain Gogol's choice of this particular symbol; he is also silent on the question of the barber Ivan Yakovlevich's role and offers no explanation for the prominence of women in the work.[7] Yet he still has no compunction about prefacing his analysis with a sharp reproof for the critic who made a serious effort to resolve these questions — Yermakov, whose well-known essay is the most extensive and searching analysis of the story that has thus far been undertaken.[8] Nor is Oulianoff alone in expressing disquiet at Yermakov's reliance on Freud and insistence that "The Nose", like Gogol's other works, is basically a dramatized confession by the author of his sexual problems. Andrey Belyy was similarly disparaging, though having declared that nothing worthwhile had yet been written about the tale, that he himself could devote an entire monograph to it and that the story "awaits its analyst", he promptly changed the subject.[9]

It follows from the general view of Gogol's art that has thus far been expressed in this study that Yermakov's recognition of the sexual implications of many details in "The Nose" and in the other stories that he examines and his perception of a recurrent opposition between masculine and feminine, or active and passive, psychological attributes are considered worthy of a very different response. At the same time it must be conceded that Yermakov is himself largely responsible for the criticism that his essays have incurred, for the value of his discoveries is repeatedly obscured by the assumptions that he derived from them. Instead of considering the possibility that the conflicting sexual characteristics that he distinguishes are no less symbolic than the details which convey them, he takes it as axiomatic that they are nothing less than the manifestations of an inner schism in the author himself and accordingly uses them as a basis for attributing to him all manner of recondite complexes. As a result, even his soundest observations have inevitably appeared questionable.

The view that will be argued in this chapter is that "The Nose" presents merely another variation, albeit the most complex that Gogol had yet composed, of the allegorical theme that lies at the basis of "Shpon'ka" and "Old-World Landowners". As stated, the first draft of the tale was written in 1833, the year in which "Old-World Landowners" was completed, and it may be noted that the beginning of the work and the text of "Old-World Landowners" were discovered in the same notebook[10] — a fact which may itself be taken to suggest a certain continuity of idea. Certainly it is not meant to imply that even on the thematic level there are no important differences between the two stories, for in at least one respect, as we shall see, the new variation of the common theme deviates significantly from the pattern that has predominated hitherto. In addition, of course, the location of the action is changed from the rural Ukraine to urban St. Petersburg. But the major difference between the two stories is clearly the more blatant disruption in "The Nose" of the balance between the two levels of the narrative. Even in "Shpon'ka" and "Old-World Landowners", as we have seen, the literal level of the text frequently defies explanation in terms of conventional logic, but the disruptions of logic are neither so numerous nor so violent as to shatter completely the illusion of normal experience. The situation in "The Nose" is plainly quite different. Here the illusion is destroyed from the outset with the discovery of the hero's nose in a loaf of bread.

It should not be thought, however, that this difference marks a fundamental change in Gogol's narrative method. It marks simply a distinctive stage in the evolution of the Gogolian two-level narrative — a stage which follows quite logically from the stages that precede it. Indeed, given the essential nature of Gogol's character-portraits, even the endowment of the hero's nose with an independent existence in the tale may be regarded as a perfectly logical development in his art. Since these portraits, as stated earlier, are essentially aggregates of symbolic motifs which convey diverse, if closely interrelated, masculine or feminine psychological characteristics, it is clear that individual motifs or groups of motifs can easily be detached for the purpose of emphasizing or more graphically representing the characteristics to which they allude. Thus in "The Two Ivans", as Yermakov has shown, the motifs which denote the attributes of a single divided personality are split into the two groups that comprise the portraits of the two main figures.[11] Similarly a collation of the motifs which comprise Chichikov's portrait and biography in chapter 11 of *Dead Souls* with those that distinguish the portraits of the five landowners in chapters 2-6 suggests that these portraits should be regarded primarily as highly detailed representations of individual facets of the hero's complex, uniquely protean personality. And since the human anatomy, in Gogol's depiction, is itself an aggregate of motifs, its constituent parts are equally liable to detachment, particularly if there is tension between the attribute signified by one particular physical feature and the other attributes of the personality. Hence the detachment from Major Kovalyov's face of the dominant symbol of his masculinity — his nose — for like that of the majority of Gogol's male characters, his masculinity is under threat from the masculinized female.

The detachment of Kovalyov's nose points forward to a particularly expressive detail which Gogol inserts in chapter 9 of *Dead Souls* into the description of the meeting between the two ladies who are intent on plotting Chichikov's downfall — namely, to the cushion adorned with the image of a knight with a flat, "ladder-like" nose which is subjected to the burden of Sof'ya Ivanovna's ample frame (VI, 180). Since Chichikov is himself likened to a knight three pages later in Sof'ya Ivanovna's account of his visit to Korobochka, the detail can only be taken to allude to the fate which they have in store for him. The assertion of female power, in other words, is to take the form of the flattening of his nose (which, as already indicated, the two ladies dislike intensely) — a vivid symbol of emasculation. It is true, of course, that the nose of Kovalyov does not share this fate; indeed, it was described in the first draft of the beginning of the story as "a masculine nose, firm and fat" (III, 380)[12] and, in the first complete version of the tale, as "firm and fleshy" (382). But although, instead of being flattened, it runs away, it is quite evident that it runs away in order to avoid being flattened. As the main symbol of the hero's masculinity, it is appropriately endowed with authoritative status — with the senior rank of

State Counsellor and a conspicuous military-type uniform (including a sword) to signify it (55); and its standing is further conveyed by several characteristic instances of Gogolian play with the differing meanings of words reminiscent of the ambiguous mode of address in Shpon'ka's letter to his aunt: by the narrator's repeated references to it as *gospodin* (54-7), which in this context suggests "master" rather than "gentleman", and by Kovalyov's decision to address it on five occasions in the cathedral as *milostivyy gosudar'* ("dear sir"/"gracious sovereign") (55-6). Yet the fugitive status of the nose is equally in evidence. "My nose," Kovalyov announces in the newspaper office, "has run away from me" (60), and its actions and experiences are clearly in harmony with his choice of verb. There is a distinctly fugitive air, for example, about its hurried, darting movements as it emerges from the carriage when Kovalyov first sees it (55); in the cathedral it tries to hide its "face" behind its military, stand-up collar (55); and it is finally apprehended with a fake passport *en route* for Riga and, implicitly, a foreign refuge.[13] The apparent objective, therefore, of this formidably attired symbol of masculine authority is to effect an escape not only from Kovalyov, but also from St. Petersburg and even from Russia itself.

The explanation of the nose's actions is indirectly suggested by the two recurrent features of Gogolian towns, and of St. Petersburg in particular, which emerge with especial clarity in *Dead Souls*. The first is the marked effeminacy of many of their menfolk, which is perhaps most clearly exemplified by the alleged talent of the governor of the town of N. for embroidering on tulle (VI, 12, 28) and which is fittingly castigated most vigorously in chapter 5 of the novel by the staunchly masculine, authoritarian Sobakevich, who significantly attributes it in large measure to foreign, mainly gallic, influence (VI, 98-9).[14] The second, complementary feature, of course, is the invariably daunting power of their female inhabitants, which is so vividly reflected in chapter 9 of the novel. Seen against this background and considered in relation to the symbolism of the nose, Kovalyov's predicament seems an entirely logical state of affairs.

Having recently arrived in the Europeanized,[15] or gallicized, metropolis from the Caucasus, where the position of the female was dictated by the Koran, the ambitious Collegiate Assessor, who, like Shpon'ka (I, 294), is in his late thirties, clearly finds himself confronted with a totally different relationship between the sexes and adapts his behaviour accordingly. With the object of advancing his career (i.e. of acquiring greater power or authority) he forsakes reliance on his own masculine instincts (as symbolised by his nose) which have thus far served him so well[16] and feels logically impelled to court the favour of the capital's most powerful citizens. As the dominant influence, therefore, on his conduct, a masculine State Counsellor is replaced by a masculinized female State Counsellor. The influence of the nose yields to that of State Counsellor Chekhtaryova and staff-officer Podtochina, whose names seem to fall from Kovalyov's lips at the merest provocation. Normally, the title of Chekhtaryova, *statskaya sovetnitsa*, would be taken to mean "State Counsellor's wife", but the notion of a "female State Counsellor" would be rendered, of course, in the same way, and the context, the significant identity of the rank with that of the nose, and the recurrence in the tale of similarly ambiguous words (for example, *gospodin* and *milostivyy gosudar'*) leave little doubt that the second meaning was meant to be implied. And since the title of Podtochina, *shtab-ofitsersha* (normally "staff-officer's wife"), is mentioned only when her name is coupled with that of Chekhtaryova, it may be inferred that it implies a similar secondary meaning, i.e. "female staff-officer", particularly as she is later attributed not only with the powers of witchcraft which betray her lineage in Gogol's fiction, but also with the ability to conduct a "battle" (*boy*) (70). It is to this female State Counsellor and female staff-officer, therefore, that Kovalyov turns for support, while the function of the "nosological" State Counsellor on his face is reduced to that of a mere embellishment to be admired in the mirror. The nose's reaction, of course, is not simply to express its indignation (in the form of a disfiguring pimple) but, in the end, to dissociate itself completely from the personality of which it formed part[17] and take to its "heels", lest it be obliged to succumb to the same objectionable influence. Apart from the various "visits" on which it embarks — for the purpose, presumably, of securing its false papers — only once does it pause in its flight: to perform the curious act of offering a prayer in the Kazan Cathedral.

The meaning of this act is suggested by the choice of church, which Gogol was clearly anxious to retain despite the predictable objections of the censorship. His reasons for choosing it may be deduced from the particular associations of the Kazan Cathedral with the war of 1812 — the war in which the French, whose ubiquitous influence on Russian urban life, as stated, is repeatedly linked by Gogol with the theme of male effeminacy, had been expelled from Russian territory. After the war the cathedral not only became a national monument to those who had fallen and the repository of captured trophies; it also housed the tomb of Kutuzov, and in 1837, i.e. one year after Gogol's completion of the redaction of "The Nose" that was published in Pushkin's journal *Sovremennik* ("The Contemporary"), monuments to Kutuzov and Barklay-de-Tolli were erected in front of it — an imminent development of which Gogol was presumably well aware. Given these military associations of the cathedral, its importance as the final resting-place of Russia's most illustrious warrior, and the repeatedly attested connection between military and "nosological" imagery in Gogol's works, it is not difficult to undersstand the attraction that the church holds for the hero's fugitive nose. Again we need to recall that military imagery not only forms a recurrent and integral part of the portraits of such male embodiments of the symbolic idea of masculinity as Taras Bul'ba, Nozdryov and Sobakevich;[18] more significantly, as we have noted, it also reappears without exception, as a symbol of their masculine past, in the biographies of Gogol's own fallen warriors, of his heroes who have been emasculated. Shpon'ka, Afanasy Ivanovich, Ivan Nikiforovich, Manilov — all served in the army before succumbing to a woman's influence and lapsing, in consequence, into a state of abject inactivity; and it may confidently be assumed that the husbands of Podtochina and Chekhtaryova have suffered a similar fate, having surrendered to their wives both the principal symbols of their masculinity (their military and Civil Service ranks) and even perhaps, like Korobochka's husband, their lives, for in the first complete redaction of "The Nose" Podtochina was explicitly referred to as a widow (396). It may readily be appreciated, therefore, why the sword-bearing nose, having witnessed, and indeed experienced, the effects of female influence on Major Kovalyov in the female-dominated realm of the capital, feels compelled to interrupt its flight. Its prayer in the cathedral is a parting act of homage to the "warriors" who have fallen in the unequal struggle — an act, it seems, which few have the courage to perform, since few have eluded the female grip. Hence the narrator's remark: "There were few people praying in the church; everyone was standing at the entrance" (55). And the same reluctance or inability to pray is appropriately displayed by the nose-less Kovalyov.

The cathedral seems to perform a directly comparable role to that of the picture-frames which enclose the portraits of Kutuzov and Peter III in chapter 3 of *Dead Souls* (VI, 47) and "Old-World Landowners" — the frames which, as symbols of confinement and control, allude to the fate of the husbands of Korobochka and Pul'kheriya Ivanovna. In precisely the same manner the implied presence of the warrior's tomb within the walls of the famous shrine in the domain of the masculinized female alludes to the fate of the capital's males. Not without cause did Gogol suggest, in a letter to Pogodin of 18 March 1835, that if the setting of the episode were to prove unacceptable to the censorship, it might be replaced by a Catholic church (X, 355). Clearly a church in which prayers are addressed to a female would have been a perfectly apt, if less expressive, substitute, an entirely fitting emblem of the symbolic "northern capital" in which Gogol places his hero. And it is equally fitting, of course, that after some indecision he should have chosen to frame the account of his hero's misfortune with the dates of Lady's Day according to the Julian and Gregorian calendars.

It may now be seen, therefore, that the arrival of an "elderly lady" in the cathedral with her alluring daughter at the precise moment when Kovalyov is striving to prevail on the nose to resume its former position (56) is by no means coincidental. The intervention is reminiscent of that of "the lady in the red dress" in "The Two Ivans" who thrusts herself forward, causing Ivan Ivanovich to fall over her, at the precise moment when the two protagonists are about to be reconciled (II, 272). It is a manifestation of the concerted female resolve to thwart the attempts of the yielding newcomer to recapture his masculine self, and its effect is exactly as intended. Instantly distracted, the major is momentarily transformed from a despairing supplicant into an entranced admirer, and on turning to readdress the nose, he predictably finds that it has gone — with its worst suspicions about the major, we may assume, significantly reinforced. And as if to re-emphasize at this moment the fate with which Kovalyov is threatened,

Gogol briefly transfers our attention to the figure of the lady's tall, hirsute footman. The important point is the highly unusual word for "footman" that he chooses — *gayduk*, which displays the same intriguing ambiguity as the words *gospodin, gosudar', statskaya sovetnitsa* and *shtab-ofitsersha*. Seemingly of Hungarian origin, the word was used to signify the partisans engaged in the struggle for freedom against the Turks in Hungary, Moldavia and the South Slavonic countries, and Gogol's awareness of this "military" source is confirmed by his use of the word in the sense of "soldier" in "Taras Bul'ba" (II, 159). At the same time it was also used in Russian to denote a footman because of the popular practice of dressing tall footmen in Hungarian uniform.[19] The word combines, therefore, the conflicting notions of "warrior" and "servant", and although the former meaning seems inadmissible in the context, Gogol immediately ensures that it will not be overlooked by portraying the *gayduk* in the act of opening his snuff-box (56) — an image which invariably in his fiction, as stated, has distinct military or, more generally, masculine connotations. It is not so much the coexistence of the two meanings that Gogol seems to be intent on conveying here as the transition from the primary to the secondary meaning, i.e. the reduction of the "warrior" to the status of servant, and in the light of the context this transition may plausibly be taken to disclose the true identity of the *gayduk*, revealing behind the mask of the footman the figure of the "elderly lady's" husband, i.e. yet another emasculated husband, another embodiment of the fate inflicted on the capital's males which alludes directly, of course, to the position of the hero. The word provides, therefore, an additional illustration of the considerable importance in the tale of *double entendres*.

The *gayduk*, however, is by no means the only animate allusion to the hero's predicament. Indeed, almost every male encountered by Kovalyov displays the same expressive ambivalence, the same contradiction between masculine facade and emasculated substance. Thus the police inspector (*kvartal'nyy nadziratel'*) who arrests the barber Ivan Yakovlevich is endowed, like the nose, with a masculine exterior that accords with his position of authority — not only with a sword and the kind of military, three-cornered hat worn by the soldiers in Plyushkin's "yellowed engraving" in chapter 6 of *Dead Souls* (VI, 115), but also with appropriate facial hirsuteness — with "broad side-whiskers" (*shirokimi bakenbardami*) (52) corresponding to the "large side-whiskers" (*bol'shimi bakenbardami*) of the *gayduk* (56). Yet when Ivan Yakovlevich, in an attempt to soften his attitude, offers unconditionally to shave him "twice or even three times" a week, he rejects the offer at once on the grounds that he already has three barbers to shave him. Are we, then, to assume that three other barbers have also sought to condition his attitude to their activities by similarly offering their services "unconditionally"? Such is the impression that we are left with until the inspector returns fifteen pages later to prompt us to reappraise his statement. After returning the nose to Kovalyov he feels obliged to request a small financial reward and pleads: "The cost of provisions has greatly increased

... At home I have my mother-in-law, that is my wife's mother, and my children" (67). Mother-in-law, wife, children — such, we may now infer, are the three "barbers", in apparent order of seniority,[20] by whom the inspector is "shaved", and given the patently masculine connotations of "hirsuteness" suggested by the portrait of Nozdryov, it can hardly be doubted, particularly after the comparison of Storchenko under female attack to "the heroes depicted by barbers on their signboards", that "to shave" in this context is "to emasculate". Hence the remark with which the inspector prefaces his revelation: "I have to go from here to the penitentiary" or, more literally, "to the house of restraint" (*v smiritel'nyy dom*) (67). The allusion is plainly to his own house with its demanding females where the word of his mother-in-law is law, and it provides an insight into the implications of the details that he includes in his description of his arrest of the nose:

> It is strange that at first I took him for a gentleman (*gospodina*), but fortunately I had my spectacles with me and I saw at once that it was a nose. I am short-sighted, you know, and if you stand in front of me I see only that you have a face, but I don't notice your nose or your beard or anything. My mother-in-law, that is my wife's mother, doesn't see anything either (66).

The passage is a graphic exposé of the inspector's emasculated personality. His normal experience, he claims, on looking at a face is to see neither nose nor beard; in other words, his "restrained masculinity" is reflected in his inability to recognize either of the two main symbols of male masculinity. But the effect of his encounter with Kovalyov's fugitive nose is momentarily to reawaken his masculinity and restore his clarity of vision, for his immediate, spontaneous reaction is to see it in the true or symbolic guise to which he is normally blind — less as a "gentleman" than as a "master". Almost at once, however, the authority of the "short-sighted" mother-in-law, whose similar inability to recognize the symbols presumably denotes an inability even to concede the existence of such a phenomenon as male masculinity, is subconsciously reasserted. The spectacles are donned and the clarity is paradoxically lost. The symbol is replaced by a meaningless lump of flesh.

The inspector, therefore, is not only a representative and upholder of the law; he is also subject to the law of his mother-in-law. The implication is clear: the law that he upholds, i.e. the law of St. Petersburg, is the law imposed by the capital's females. Thus our interpretation of the nose's motive for fleeing is notably reinforced, and it seems fitting that its escape should be thwarted by this particular agent of female power. In order to ensure, however, that the indicated implication of the inspector's portrait is recognized as a general comment on the capital's police, Gogol reiterates it by introducing two additional policemen into the tale. It is true that one of them — the chief of police (*oberpolitsmeyster*) — does not appear at all, but his absence, which reminds us of Storchenko's absence when Vasilisa Kashporovna visits his estate, is precisely the point. The disappearance of the capital's principal representative of male authority a few seconds before the hero arrives to enlist his assistance in the task of recovering his masculinity immediately suggests that the chief is just as susceptible to subconscious promptings as the hapless inspector. "He has just left ...", announces the door-keeper. "If you had come a moment earlier, you would perhaps have caught him at home" (58). Like the intervention of the "elderly lady" in the cathedral and Kovalyov's inability to find a single cab on the street when he first sallies forth in quest of the nose (54), the chief's sudden departure is another indication of the uncanny, all-embracing character of female control over life in the capital and provides additional evidence that the hero, like Storchenko, is unwittingly the victim of a weird conspiracy. Having "restrained" the newcomer to the extent of parting him from his nose, the city's genuine authorities are clearly determined that the separation will be permanent. But the distinctive feature, of course, of the plot of "The Nose" is that in this case, as the restoration of the nose to its former position testifies, the female conspiracy fails, and it is here that we encounter one of the major ironies of the work, for it is precisely the emasculation of the police that causes the failure. Before the nose can be restored, it has to be recovered, and its recovery is ensured by the mark of emasculation that distinguishes the inspector — by the "short-sightedness" that prompts him to don the spectacles which render him incapable of distinguishing noses as symbols from noses as flesh. Acting in obedience to the promptings of his domestic "chief" (his mother-in-law), he ironically frustrates their central purpose.

The third member of the emasculated police force to whom Kovalyov turns for assistance is the police superintendent (*chastnyy pristav*), who responds with a refusal which is no longer implicit, like that of the chief, but completely unequivocal. The explanation is again to be perceived in the details of the portrait, which reflect the same contradiction as that which lies at the basis of the inspector's portrait — the contradiction conveyed by Gogol's oft-quoted comment on St. Petersburg in "The Nevsky Prospect": "Everything is a deception, everything is a dream, everything is other than it seems" (49). Indeed, the contradiction is expressed with remarkable conciseness by the descriptive phrase with which the portrait begins: "a lover of sugar" (*okhotniku do sakharu*) (63). Rejected by the censorship, presumably on the grounds of its irreverence, the phrase presents yet another example of the kind of problem with which the translator of Gogol's works is repeatedly confronted — the usually insuperable problem, illustrated by the noun *gayduk*, of devising a translation that conveys two quite different meanings simultaneously. In addition to "lover" or "enthusiast", the noun *okhotnik* means "hunter" and thus reintroduces the symbolic indicator of the masculine mentality that we have encountered in the portraits of Shpon'ka's aunt, Nozdryov and Mikita (in "Viy"). Even the vestigial masculinity of Afanasy Ivanovich in "Old-World Landowners" manifests itself, as we have observed, in a momentary reawakening of his passion for the hunt. Naturally enough, when the nouns *okhotnik* and *okhota* are encountered in portraits of this kind, the translations "hunter" and "hunting" are normally demanded by the context, but even when the literal context demands the translations "lover" (or "enthusiast") and "desire", the symbolic context of the portraits concerned leaves little doubt that the alternative notions are fully implicit. It can hardly be considered coincidence, for example, that in the context of the chapter of *Dead Souls* which is wholly devoted to the portrait of the "hunter" Nozdryov Chichikov negates the noun *okhotnik* (in the literal sense of "lover"), instead of the verb *lyubit'* ("to like"), to express his dislike of playing cards, thereby prompting two immediate repetitions of the noun which seem designed to suggest that there is rather more to the word than meets the eye.[21] Expressing on one level his dislike of card-games, Chichikov implies on another his reluctance to expose himself to the ruthless, unprincipled masculinity of the pugnacious "hunter".

We may conclude, therefore, on this basis that the superintendent is not only a "lover" but also a "hunter" and, as such, an apparent embodiment of the masculine virtues. But the appearance is immediately undermined by the reference to the object of his "love": he is a "lover-cum-hunter" of "sugar" — an image, as we have noted in connection with Vasilisa Kashporovna's fruit-gathering and jam-boiling activities, with distinctly "feminine" associations which emerge most clearly in the simile of the "sugar loaf" in chapter 1 of *Dead Souls* and in the portrait of the effeminate Manilov.[22] It may be argued, therefore, that the essential meaning of the phrase *okhotniku do sakharu* is: masculine (i.e. a hunter) in appearance, emasculated (i.e. a lover of females) in reality, and the subsequent details of the superintendent's portrait serve clearly to substantiate this conclusion. Not only does he share the enthusiasm of Manilov and the governor of the town of N. for "all arts and artifacts" (63), but at the precise moment when Kovalyov enters his house the female cook is in the process of vigorously stripping him of his masculine emblems:

> At this moment the cook was throwing off the superintendent's official jackboots; his sword and all his military armour (*voennyye dospekhi*) had already been hung peacefully in the corners, and his three-year-old son had already begun to finger his menacing three-cornered hat; and after the martial life of a warrior he was preparing to partake of the pleasure of peace (63).

The scene is reminiscent not only of the partly stripped figure of the perspiring Storchenko, but also of the spectacle that greets the eyes of Ivan Ivanovich in chapter 2 of "The Two Ivans" — the spectacle of Ivan Nikiforovich's uniform and weapons being hung on the clothes-line by a "skinny woman" (II, 228-30); and once more we are reminded of the readiness with which Chichikov in chapter 3 of *Dead Souls* surrenders his "wet armour" (*mokryye dospekhi*) to

Korobochka's maid Fetin'ya (VI, 47). The four scenes present four variations of the same symbolic motif — the motif of "stripping" which is plainly an extension of the motif of "shaving".[23] Just as the nose of Kovalyov has been put to flight by Chekhtaryova (whose name is probably derived from the noun *chekhor* ("pugnacious person or ruffian")) and Podtochina (whose name is derived from the verb *podtochit'* which means "to sap, undermine"), so the masculine vitality of the superintendent has been "sapped" by his domestic "barbers". All that remains is a profound need for peace and sleep, for the same soporific tranquillity that is sought by Storchenko after his defiant mutilation of the hen and in which the emasculated spirit of Afanasy Ivanovich languishes behind the palisade which is the wall of his prison.[24]

The three policemen, therefore, play two distinct but closely related roles in the story. On the one hand, their portraits allude to the usurpation of authority by the capital's females and thus explain the narrator's choice of the first of the two urban landmarks that he mentions when describing the scene that confronts Kovalyov on the Nevsky Prospect as he emerges from the cathedral: "Ladies were scattered like a waterfall of flowers over the whole pavement from the police headquarters to the Anichkin Bridge" (57). On the other hand, like the reference to the *gayduk*, the portraits allude to the hero's dilemma. In this respect the portrait of the superintendent is particularly informative, for by illuminating the role of the motif of sleep as a metaphor of emasculation it indirectly explains the condition of the hero at the moment when we first meet him: he is in bed. Just as the policemen, however, are not the only figures in whom the hero's fate is paralleled, so they are not the only male participants in the female conspiracy. Equally clear indications of involvement, for example, are immediately apparent in the portrait of the clerk in the newspaper office, whose habit of taking snuff from a box with a lid that displays "the portrait of a lady in a hat" (63) is yet another symbolic reflection of the contradiction expressed by the phrase *okhotniku do sakharu* in the portrait of the superintendent. Once more a female presence overshadows a masculine symbol, implicitly explaining not only the clerk's rejection of the major's appeal, but also the excuse that he offers. As a parallel to Kovalyov's advertisement he cites, to the major's astonishment, the case of an advertisement recently brought by a government clerk which announced the loss of "a poodle with a black coat" — a poodle which ultimately, he adds, turned out to be "the cashier of some department" (61), i.e. presumably an official who had absconded with the departmental funds. The image of the dog, the black coat, the reckless pursuit of gain — every detail in the silhouette of the poodle-cashier anticipates once more the portrait of the "nosey", reckless, black-whiskered Nozdryov, and it may be noted that the poodle in the story of the clerk, like the nose in the story of Kovalyov less than a page earlier, "ran away"; the same verb (*sbezhal*) is used in both accounts (60-1). Between the nose and the poodle, therefore, we perceive a perfectly apt parallel between different symbols of the same mentality — a mentality which in the capital is anathema in the male and thus an improper subject for a respectable newspaper. Having earned the rebukes of the readership — more precisely, we may assume, of the female readership — for printing the earlier advertisement, the clerk is understandably loath to repeat his mistake. But there can be little doubt that he will not be so reluctant to advertise the loss of another dog — that of the countess whose footman addresses Kovalyov in the queue:

> Would you believe it, sir, the little cur isn't worth eighty copecks; in fact, I wouldn't give eight half-copecks for it. But the countess is fond of it — my goodness, she's fond of it — and there are a hundred roubles for the man who finds it. If one may speak with propriety, as you and I are speaking now, people's tastes are quite incompatible: thus if you're a hunter (*okhotnik*), then keep a setter or a poodle; you won't mind spending five hundred or even a thousand provided it's a good dog (59).

Here the familiar images of hunter and hunting hound duly reappear to highlight by contrast the emasculation of the countess's diminutive canine subject (*sobachonka*), which provides additional animate testimony to the debilitating effects of female power.

Instead of assistance the clerk offers advice, and Kovalyov eventually takes it: after the nose has been apprehended and returned to him by the "short-sighted" inspector he calls in a doctor. The result, however, merely clarifies the clerk's motive for making the suggestion, for the doctor predictably turns out to be yet another obedient male tool. Yet again the image of Nozdryov is evoked by the doctor's physical portrait — by the references to his glowing health, "fine pitch-black whiskers" and shining white teeth (68), and there is perhaps even a hint of Nozdryov's addiction to physical violence in the obvious relish with which the doctor flicks the smooth plateau between the major's cheeks. But while the wife of Nozdryov is speedily hastened to her grave, the wife of the doctor is "fresh and healthy" (68) and in consequence, we may deduce, admirably equipped for the task of "shaving". Once more, therefore, a contrasting reality is sensed behind the masculine appearance, and the major's appeal is accordingly futile. Just as the clerk foresees "no advantage" in advertising the loss of the nose (62), so the doctor predicts harmful effects if he attempts to reattach it (69). The comments of both counsellors seem to reflect a profound awareness, doubtless born of personal experience, that to flaunt a nose in the world of the capital is to invite a painful riposte. The recommended treatment, therefore, is frequent washings of the nose in cold water and immersion in spirit or, "better still", in pungent vodka or heated vinegar (69). The implications of this advice will become abundantly clear in the light of the imagery of chapter 1.

The portraits of the doctor and spokesman for the press are directly related to those of the three policemen in the sense that while the latter portraits imply female control of the capital's law, the former imply the same control over the minds and bodies of its inhabitants. Taken together, therefore, the five portraits may be viewed as a composite allusion to the comprehensiveness of female authority, and it accordingly comes as no surprise to find that the symptoms of emasculation are no less clearly marked even in the briefly sketched silhouettes of males which flash by rapidly in the background. In each case the procedure is the same: the identification of the figure concerned with a particular masculine symbol which in some respect is flawed or nullified. Although, for example, the head clerk Yarygin, who makes a fleeting appearance on the Nevsky Prospect, is graced with an emphatically masculine name suggestive of ardour and violence, he also enjoys a reputation for incompetence in the masculine activity of card-playing (57). Similarly the associate whom Kovalyov is given to addressing as lieutenant-colonel turns out, in reality, to be a Court Counsellor (57). Here, as in the portrait of Kovalyov himself who calls himself "Major" but is actually a Collegiate Assessor, the military rank corresponding to the Civil Service rank suggests a spurious masculinity, a masculine appearance concealing an emasculated reality.

Only once in the tale, in fact, does Gogol introduce an inhabitant of the capital who is a genuine military man, and appropriately his masculinity, it seems, is completely authentic and unimpaired. The figure in question is the "honoured colonel" who leaves home early, we are told, for the express purpose of catching sight of the militarily attired nose, which is aptly rumoured to have been spotted in "Junker's shop" (72). For the colonel, it seems, the nose's appearance represents a rare opportunity to make contact with a kindred spirit, with a fellow rebel against the prevailing order. But on his arrival, he discovers "to his profound indignation" not only that the nose has departed, but also that it had good reason for departing:

> ... instead of the nose he saw in the window of the shop the usual woollen jersey and a lithograph depicting a girl adjusting her stocking, while a dandy with a small beard in a waistcoat with lapels was peering at her from behind a tree ... (72).

Even Mr. Junker, therefore, has apparently succumbed to female enticement, for there can be little doubt that the enraptured dandy is meant to be viewed as a projection of the proprietor himself who has exchanged his junker's "armour" for an effeminate waistcoat and an abbreviated beard. Hence the nose's departure and the colonel's wrath.

The alleged appearance of the nose in "Junker's shop" is merely one of several rumours circulating in the capital which combine to evoke the impression of a persecuted beast. The succession of locations in which it is sighted conveys the rapidity of its movements as it switches from point to point in a desperate and vain endeavour to find a breach in the wall. It seems fitting, therefore, that when the "beast" is eventually obliged to seek refuge in the Tavrichesky

Garden,[25] it should be hotly pursued by students of the Surgical Academy and noted with interest by Hozrev-Mirza, the envoy of the alien people by whom the dramatist Griboyedov, in the capacity of Russian Minister to Persia, was stoned to death (72). And the same interest is naturally displayed by the capital's females as represented by the "distinguished and respectable lady" who is anxious that her children should witness the spectacle and be furnished with "an edifying and instructive explanation" (72) — presumably to the effect that such is the penalty for following one's nose. The reaction of those obedient males who are not actually engaged in the pursuit varies from that of the "inveterate visitors of social gatherings and devoted entertainers of the ladies", for whom the rumours of the fugitive's adventures are merely a welcome supplementary source of amusing anecdotes, to that of the "gentleman" (*gospodin*) who is appalled that such "absurd fictions" are permitted to circulate and demands the intervention of the government — "one of those gentlemen (*gospod*)," the narrator adds, "who would like to involve the government in everything, even in their daily quarrels with their wives" (72). Little do they appreciate, it seems, that given the nature of the capital's genuine government, neither their status as *gospoda* nor their ability to "quarrel" would survive its intervention.

With the exception of the colonel, therefore, every male in the story bears the mark of complete or partial emasculation and, with the additional exception of the hero, is accordingly antagonistic to the fleeing nose or indifferent to its misfortunes. For Kovalyov, however, the recovery of his nose is almost literally a matter of life and death,[26] and this anxiety to be rejoined with the fugitive can only signify that despite the unequivocal evidence of his emasculation, his state of mind has as much in common with that of the colonel as with that of the capital's other males. Like almost every other male in the work, therefore, the major displays an intriguing ambivalence, but this is clearly ambivalence of a different order, for now external evidence of emasculation is contradicted by the evidence of actions and aspirations.

The flight of Kovalyov's nose, as stated, is presented less as a symptom of his emasculation than as a consequence of it, and the more obvious explanations of its flight have already been noted: his deference to certain influential ladies, especially Podtochina, who perceives in him a potential son-in-law; his treatment of his nose as a mere embellishment and generally effeminate preoccupation with his appearance; and the falsity of his military rank. It has also been observed that he first presents himself to the reader in bed, and therefore "stripped", and we learn that twice a week he submits to a shave. Each of these details and aspects of his conduct alludes to his incipient surrender to the capital's emasculating influence. The most conclusive evidence, however, has yet to be considered. It is to be found in chapter 1 in the figure of the barber.

The judgment that Ivan Yakovlevich is "another face of Kovalyov himself" has already been expressed by Yermakov, though few, one imagines, would agree with his interpretation of this "face".[27] The suggestion, of course, places little strain on credulity, for it seems perfectly reasonable to suppose that having detached one aspect of the hero's personality in the form of the nose, Gogol might well have been disposed to detach another in a different guise. But more substantial support for the view is offered by the three pieces of intrinsic evidence that Yermakov adduces: the identical positions of the two characters when they are first introduced (they are both in bed, i.e. drained of vitality); the absence of any explicit reference to Ivan Yakovlevich's nose; and the notion of one complete name suggested by the barber's Christian name and patronymic and the hero's surname. It is true that for reasons that will become clear shortly Kovalyov is later endowed with a distinct Christian name and patronymic (Platon Kuz'mich), but they emerge only in his exchange of letters with Podtochina. With this exception, he is known throughout the tale exclusively by his surname. Even more cogent evidence, however, of the relationship between the two characters is provided by a connection between their names that has not been detected. The patronymic "Yakovlevich" was selected by Gogol only after considerable thought, for it was preceded in the first draft of the beginning of the tale by "Ivanovich" (380) and in the first complete redaction by "Fyodoro-vich" (381). Since the third choice was presumably considered by the author to be an improvement on its predecessors, it seems reasonable to enquire into his reasons for preferring it. The merest glance at it provides the answer, for truncation of the suffix ("ich") and initial *yod* ("y") leaves all the elements of the name "Kovalev" (which has been rendered as "Kovalyov" simply because of the convention of transliterating the Russian vowel *ë* as "yo"). The only difference is the displacement of the middle vowel ("a"), which may seem to weaken the argument until we recall the displacement of the middle feature on the major's face. If it is granted, therefore, that the echo is not simply coinci-dence, the "deformed" patronymic may be taken to signify not only that Ivan Yakovlevich is the hero's offspring or creation (which would explain the ease with which he recognizes the nose), but also that he is the embodiment of the "deformity" that has caused the displacement. In other words, as the symbolism of his profession additionally suggests, he is the embodiment of the weakness in the hero against which the nose has rebelled, the cause incarnate of the nose's flight, and since causes precede effects, the barber logically dominates the opening chapter.

The order, however, in which the characters are presented also seems to carry an additional implication which makes it possible to determine the role of Ivan Yakovlevich with somewhat greater precision. As indicated, both characters are introduced to the reader in the act of waking from sleep — first the barber, then the major — and since the first stirrings of consciousness are normally preceded in sleep by subconscious activity, it seems plausible to conjecture that this anticipatory activity of the subconscious is precisely the content of chapter 1. The sequence of chapters 1 and 2, in short, seems to convey the waking of the two levels of the hero's personality — first the subconscious level (Ivan Yakovlevich — Christian name and patronymic), and then the conscious level (Kovalyov — surname). This is not to suggest, of course, the the events of chapter 1 are presented as a dream. Like the flight of the nose, they are presented as an objective reality, and this seems entirely fitting inasmuch as the workings of the subconscious are largely unknown to the conscious mind. Hence the apparent lack of connection between chapters 1 and 2, Kovalyov's refusal to link the disappearance of his nose with Ivan Yakovlevich, and his distinct Christian name and patronymic. Unconscious of the cause, which lies deeply buried in his personality, he is totally mystified by the effect.

The story begins, therefore, with a dramatic incision into the hero's "stinking" subconscious[28] which provides the insight into his true self that explains his experiences on waking, and appropriately the descent to a lower level of the mind is reflected in a descent to a lower social level. Here Kovalyov exists in the guise of the squalid barber who has cut off his nose and let his blood — actions that symbolise a subconscious surrender to female power which has "undermined" or "sapped" his masculine vitality. Hence the portrayal of the barber as the intimidated subject of a "sturdy spouse" (as she was described in an earlier draft (380)) — the formidable Praskov'ya Osipovna, who is not only similarly devoid of a surname, but likewise has a surnamed counterpart in chapters 2 and 3 whose identity in similar manner is disclosed by her patronymic, for its vowels are the vowels of the surname "Podtochina" which, like the vowels of "Kovalev" in the patronymic "Yakovlevich", are reproduced in due sequence but for a single metathesis. The implication is again self-evident: Praskov'ya Osipovna is the image of Podtochina that resides in the hero's subconscious, while her status as wife and appropriation of masculine power reflect his subconscious awareness of the threat that Podtochina embodies. Herein lies the explanation of his later, seemingly illogical conviction that Podtochina is the cause of his woes (65). The truth known to the subconscious is suddenly elevated to the level of consciousness.

The true "barber" of Kovalyov, therefore, is not so much his subconscious self, in the form of Ivan Yakovlevich, as Podtochina in the guise of Praskov'ya Osipovna, and the details which comprise her brief portrait in chapter 1 relate her unmistakably to the most notable female "barbers" in Gogol's fiction. Not only is she intent on depriving her victim of such stimulating beverages as coffee, to which she is personally addicted[29]; like Shpon'ka's aunt, Storchenko's mother, Pul'kheriya Ivanovna and the female who divests the superintendent, she is also cast in the ominous role of cook, being introduced to the reader in the act of removing "newly baked loaves (*khleby*)" from the oven (49). Considered in relation to the parallel images in Gogol's other works — particularly in relation to the narrator's remark in *Dead Souls* that Sobakevich, during the negotiations with Chichikov, referred to his dead souls "as if the subject of conversation were bread (*khlebe*)" (VI, 101) — these products of Praskov'ya Osipovna's activity admit of only one interpretation: the loaves that she bakes are metaphors of

Ivan Yakovlevich's emasculated soul and, as such, explain her later reference to him as a *sukhar' podzharistyy* (50) — a phrase used metaphorically to signify "a dried-up person" which means literally "a burnt rusk". While the "baking" of Afanasy Ivanovich, as we have seen, in the pressure-cooker of Pul'kheriya Ivanovna's "little house" is actually shown, that of Kovalyov's *alter ego* is conveyed exclusively by symbol, and in the light of this symbolism we may now comprehend the implications not only of the comparison of the smooth space between the major's cheeks to a "baked pancake" (62), but also of the doctor's advice when he recommends immersing the nose in pungent vodka and "heated vinegar". The baking of the loaves, in short, would seem to complement the symbolism of the name "Podtochina". It is a symbolic illustration of the process of "sapping".

Clearly the crucial point, however, is that the process of baking, as in the Foreword to "Shpon'ka", is only partly successful, for it is survived by the hero's most potent masculine instincts in the form of the nose, just as it is survived by the most important part of Stepan Ivanovich Kurochka's manuscript. Hence the indignation of Praskov'ya Osipovna when the loaf discloses its contents. Subconsciously Kovalyov has yielded and been transformed, in the person of Ivan Yakovlevich, into a newly baked loaf, but in the face of the female oppressor his instincts assert themselves and ultimately emerge unscathed from the oven's heat. Indeed, in the first complete redaction of the story the nose was specifically described as "cold" (382), and it may now be appreciated why Kovalyov's later attempts to make it stick by "heating it slightly with his breath" (68) are unsuccessful.

The coexistence of the nose and the loaf, therefore, would appear to parallel the coexistence of the nose and Ivan Yakovlevich as contrasting symbols of the hero's ambivalence or duality. Yet the situation is plainly more complex than this, for Ivan Yakovlevich is not only contrasted with the nose; he is also part of the same personality, and the nose is actually discovered within the loaf which is a symbolic extension of his portrait. In other words, the element of ambivalence is clearly perceptible even in the barber himself, and it is only in the light of this fact that the wrath of his wife and her refusal to intercede on his behalf with the police (i.e. with the capital's female-dominated police) become fully intelligible. It also explains a number of other details in his portrait, which similarly suggest that his masculine instincts are still alive: his reluctance to dispose of the nose; the detail in his physical portrait of his "continually unshaved chin" (51); his liking for snuff; the introduction of the noun *okhota* into the description of him shaving Kovalyov (51); and his habit of tugging so vigorously at the noses of his clients that he almost dislodges them — a habit that can only be taken to allude to his desire to compensate for the loss of his own nose by appropriating the noses of others. Viewed from this angle, therefore, the barber's professional activities acquire a new dimension of meaning.

In the end, however, his desire to be reintegrated with the nose proves to be less compelling than his fear of Praskov'ya Osipovna. Submitting to her will and endeavouring to conceal his burden from the eyes of the capital's emasculated police, he makes for the Neva and casts it into its waters. The method of disposal is itself worthy of note, for it seems to point forward not only to the doctor's advice to Kovalyov — specifically to his first recommendation: that he wash his nose regularly in cold water — but also to the comparison of the ladies on the Nevsky Prospect to a "waterfall". The image of water has a particular resonance in Gogol's fiction and, like so many of his images, can perhaps be traced back to "Shpon'ka" — to the image of "the Flood" that is woven into the description of Vasilisa Kashporovna's chaise.[30] At the same time the genesis of the image may conceivably be linked with an inhabitant of the folk-tale world of the other stories of *Evenings* — namely, the mermaid (*rusalka*), whose eyes, according to the narrator of "A Terrible Vengeance", "entice the soul from a man", whose bed "is cold water" and who "will tickle you and drag you into the river" (I, 274),[31] thus reminding us of Korobochka's habit of tickling her husband's heels (VI, 47) while dragging him to his death in the muddy fields of her rain-soaked domain. However that may be, the image of water seems to be almost invariably associated in Gogol's works with the extinction of such masculine or "Nozdryovian" attributes as passion, vitality and ebullience. Thus in "The Two Ivans" Ivan Nikiforovich, who becomes so curiously passive in the presence of the bellicose Agafiya Fedoseyevna, has his symbolic gun washed and hung on the clothes-line (II, 230) and develops the intriguing habit of drinking tea in a pool of water (II, 227). But the meaning of the image is perhaps most vividly disclosed by the famous passage in chapter 6 of *Dead Souls* in which Plyushkin's inability to register feeling on his "wooden face" prompts the narrator to compare him to a drowning man (VI, 126), and it is in the light of this passage that we may consider the choice of imagery in "The Nose" when the narrator describes the contrast between Kovalyov's joy on recovering his nose and his grief on being unable to restore it to its proper position:

> But nothing in this world is of long duration, and so his joy a moment later was not so great. After another moment had passed it became even weaker and finally merged imperceptibly with the usual state of his soul, just as a circle on the water caused by a falling stone finally merges with the smooth surface (*gladkoyu poverkhnost'yu*) (67).

The simile plainly alludes to the dropping of the nose in the capital's river, the result of which is the "smooth space" (*gladkoye mesto*) (53) between the major's cheeks.

There is good reason, therefore, to suppose that the casting of the nose in the Neva is yet another symbolic portrayal of the process of emasculation, and given Gogol's liking for the conventional image of fire as a symbol of the human spirit, the logical basis of the image is not difficult to perceive. Alluding to the extinction of the "flame" of masculine vitality, the image of water may be coupled with the image of heat as one of the most recurrent of the symbolic indicators which convey the emasculation of the Gogolian male by the Gogolian female.[32] Hence, perhaps, the name of the "sober" suitor who, according to Podtochina's letter to Kovalyov (71), had sought the hand of her daughter – Filipp Ivanovich Potanchikov, whose surname, which is probably derived from the Ukrainian verb *potanuti* ("to sink"), suggests that his "sobriety" may be attributed to the fact that he has been thoroughly immersed in metaphorical water. Still more significant, however, in this connection is the name of Podtochina herself – or, more precisely, the erroneous Christian name that Kovalyov bestows on her. Although her signature beneath her letter reveals her name to be Aleksandra Grigor'yevna (71), he refers to her in his exchanges with the newspaper clerk as Pelageya Grigor'yevna (60), thus giving her a Christian name which, like her patronymic, is derived from a highly expressive Greek root. Echoing that of Storchenko and the sacristan of the Dikan'ka church, the patronymic, signifying "vigilance" or "wakefulness", implicitly attributes her with the masculine energy and vitality which are so conspicuously lacking in the dormant hero to whom we are first introduced. It may accordingly be related to the fact that Praskov'ya Osipovna, Kovalyov's subconscious image of Podtochina, has already completed her baking by the time that Ivan Yakovlevich wakes up. At the same time the Christian name, derived from the adjective *pelagios* ("of the sea"), associates her with the image of water which expresses the idea of the extinction of such energy in the male. It may be deduced, therefore, that the name "Pelageya" is intended to convey Kovalyov's subconscious notion of the means by which Podtochina has "sapped" his masculine energy, i.e. to the immersion of the nose in the Neva. His use of the "incorrect" name may be directly related to his similarly "illogical" supposition at a later stage in the narrative that Podtochina is responsible for his misfortune; indeed, it may be viewed as an anticipatory signal of this supposition in the sense that it represents a preliminary response of his conscious mind to subconscious prompting.

Podtochina and Potanchikov, however, are not the only characters in the work to be endowed with names that may be connected with the image of water. Thus in the light of the extensive play with names in this story, we may be tempted to see more than coincidence in the fact that, with the exception once more of a single metathesis, the Christian name (Ivan) of the major's barber, i.e. of the animate symbol of that part of his personality which has been "immersed in water", is a phonetic rendering of the noun "Neva". And it may be observed that the same Christian name is also bestowed on Kovalyov's servant, whose lack of energy is immediately apparent in the recumbent posture from which he is given to spitting at the ceiling (64). The implications of this pastime perhaps become apparent if we consider the name in relation to another detail in the description of the nose's immersion — namely, to the reference to Ivan Yakovlevich's search for fish before he drops it into the Neva (51-2). If water is indeed a symbolic emasculating agent, it seems reasonable to regard the fish as symbolic victims of its emasculating powers, and since Ivan Yakovlevich, impelled by fear of the consequences if he should be discovered in possession of such an expressive symbol of male masculinity as a nose, is intent, above all, on concealment, his interest in the whereabouts of the fish seems entirely natural. Where better, it may be asked, to conceal a symbol of masculinity than among symbols of the emasculated?[33] Perhaps we may regard, therefore, the curious pastime of Ivan the servant as a symbolic indicator of his emasculated condition, as presenting an arresting analogy to the spectacle of a fish on dry land pumping water from its body. Not only is he recumbent, i.e. deficient in vitality; by both his name and his actions he is linked, on the one hand, with the Neva and, on the other, with Ivan Yakovlevich. His portrayal as fish, if our interpretation is correct, corresponds directly to the portrayal of Ivan Yakovlevich as loaf, while his role as servant parallels the latter's role as barber, for just as Ivan Yakovlevich strips the hero of his whiskers, so Ivan the servant strips him of his clothes (in addition to supplying him with the vodka with which he wipes his chin after shaving (65), thus reminding us once more of the recommendation of the doctor). Thus when Kovalyov enters his apartment, Ivan, we read, "suddenly leapt up from his place and rushed headlong to take off his cloak" (64). The scene clearly recalls the disrobing of the superintendent, which takes place only one page earlier, and seems to confirm that this second Ivan should be viewed as a second symbol of the hero's subconscious — as another precursor of the indolent Petrushka in *Dead Souls* who daily disrobes the "nosey" Chichikov.

Having disposed of the nose and been apprehended by the inspector, Ivan Yakovlevich fades from the scene, and the whole incident, in the narrator's phrase, "is enveloped in a mist" (52). Such is the means by which Gogol conveys the transition to a different level of the mind, the retreat of the subconscious before the onset of consciousness, and the link is indicated at once, in the first sentence of chapter 2, by the sound that emerges from the major's lips as he opens his eyes — the sound 'brr . . .", which would appear to be a reaction to the temperature, but may also be taken to denote a semi-conscious memory of the barber's razor (*britva*). From this moment onward until the end of chapter 2 the effects of the razor's work, as we have observed, are manifest in almost all the major's actions. Indeed, during his visit to the newspaper office even his surname is briefly "shaved off", like that of Ivan Yakovlevich. Instead of revealing it to the clerk he mentions only his acquaintance with Chekhtaryova and Podtochina, i.e. with the females who have "shaved" him, and the surname is aptly assumed at this moment of weakness by the aliented embodiment of his masculinity, the nose (*nos*), which is referred to by the clerk as "Mr. (*gospodin*) Nosov" (60).

Even so, it is clear from the outset that the newcomer from the Caucasus is destined to survive the ordeal to which the capital subjects him. The prospect of resurrection is indicated immediately, in the second sentence of the story, by the location of Ivan Yakovlevich's shop — Voznesensky ("Ascension") Prospect (49),[34] and it is again suggested one page later by the notification that he shaved the major "every Sunday", i.e. on the weekly "resurrection day" (*voskresen'ye*). Moreover, although both the major and his *alter ego* are first portrayed in bed, they are nevertheless, as stated, in the process of "waking up". In the end, of course, the realisation of the prediction conveyed by these details is marked not by the return of the nose, for it returns against its will (as evidenced by its still prominent pimple (67)), but by its restoration, now without the pimple, to its proper position on the major's face (73), and the reason for its restoration is clearly suggested by the sequence of events. Having been "miraculously" returned to the major immediately after his conception of the thought that his misfortune is the work of Podtochina (65-6), the nose dutifully resumes its position in the wake of the action that he takes in response to this thought — namely, the dispatch of his letter. Conscious identification of the source of danger is followed by decisive action against it — action which implicitly convinces the nose that it is safe to return. The letter should be read, therefore, as testimony to the major's readiness, if necessary, to engage his adversary in battle, as evidence of a reborn determination to reassert his masculinity in the face of the "female staff-officer's" attempts to emasculate him. It is true that he still displays his ignorance of the scale of the forces mounted against him by threatening to refer the case to the law, but he leaves Podtochina in no doubt about the futility of her insidious assault: "You may be sure that you will gain nothing by acting in this manner, and you will in no way force me to marry your daughter" (70).

In her reply, of course, Podtochina professes surprise at his charges, but again it is necessary to take note of the two levels on which the dialogue is conducted. When she remarks: "Your letter greatly surprised me. I frankly confess that I in no way expected it ..." (70), she is expressing, in reality, her surprise at the resilience of this newcomer who had seemed to be on the verge of surrender. Hence her reference at this point to Potanchikov, whom she seems to confuse with the nose in its guise as State Counsellor: "It is true that Filipp Ivanovich Potanchikov has been to see me, and although, indeed, he sought the hand of my daughter and is a sober man of good behaviour and great learning, I never gave him any hope" (71). In the figure of this "sunken" suitor we may now recognize a symbolic embodiment of the "sober" condition to which, in the eyes of Podtochina, the major's masculinity (in the form of the nose) had been irreversibly reduced — a condition which had seemed to her to offer "no hope" of recovery. The effect of the major's letter is at once to disabuse her of this impression, thereby perhaps confirming the connection indicated by Yermakov between the name "Kovalyov" and the verb *podkovat'* ("to deceive"),[35] and to highlight the necessity of renewing the attack. Dismissing the thought of Potanchikov, she now addresses herself to the subject of the nose:

You also mention a nose. If you mean by this that I wished to dupe you (*ostavit' vas s nosom*), i.e. to give you a formal refusal, it surprises me that you should say such a thing, for, as you well know, I was minded to do the precise opposite, and if you will now court my daughter in a lawful manner, I am ready to satisfy you at once, for this has always been the object of my keenest desires . . . (71).

As in the case of the noun *gayduk*, a secondary or metaphorical meaning is again employed to cloak a crucial primary meaning. While declaring that she had no intention of "duping" the major, Podtochina is literally saying that she had no intention of "leaving him with his nose", and her renewed pressure on him to marry her daughter reconfirms her commitment to the same objective.

Like the males of the town of N. in *Dead Souls*, Kovalyov, of course, is no match for such subtle female guile and immediately accepts the letter as evidence of Podtochina's innocence. Yet his gullibility is of little consequence. Though now convinced that his suspicion was unjustified, he has nevertheless demonstrated his ability to withstand the assault of even the most determined female oppressor, and at the beginning of chapter 3 the "smooth space" is gladly reoccupied by the reassured nose. Almost at once the two Ivans alight on the scene to register a subconscious protest, but now neither the servant's water nor the barber's razor has the power to propel the nose into renewed flight. Protected by the major's command from the barber's eager fingers,[36] it resolutely stands its ground, and the narrative ends with a sequence of vivid illustrations of the effects of its return. Now the capital becomes the stage on which the major parades his recovered masculinity. He mocks the nose of a passing soldier which is "no bigger than a waistcoat button" (74); in a manner reminiscent of the scornful gesture of the *panich* from Poltava in *Evenings* (I, 106-7) he ostentatiously packs both his nostrils with snuff in the presence of Podtochina, adding under his breath: "So much for you, you womenfolk, you hens!" (74); and he succumbs to the lure of the capital's "pretty ladies" no longer as a potential victim, but as a "pursuer" (or "hunter") (75). The final page of the narrative is a record of the hero's triumph, and it perhaps casts some light on the reasons for Gogol's choice of 23 April as the date on which the action of the tale took place in the version published by *Sovremennik* in 1836, for 23 April is the feast day of St. George. In the final version we may perhaps discern a reflection of this abandoned allusion in the last act of the major before we leave him — in his purchase of "the ribbon of some order" from the capital's main emporium (75). Elevation to the Order of St. George seems an entirely fitting reward for a solitary conqueror of the capital's dragons and, naturally enough in a society that is dominated by dragons, only the conqueror himself can bestow it. As the narrator remarks in the ironic epilogue: "Whatever anyone might say, such things do happen in the world — not often, but they do happen" (75).

With these concluding words Gogol underlines the rarity of the phenomenon in which the events of his tale culminate — the phenomenon of male triumph which constitutes the major departure from the thematic pattern that lies at the basis of almost all his preceding works. Only the victories of Levko in "A May Night" and Stepan Ivanovich Kurochka can be said to anticipate the outcome of Kovalyov's adventure. Yet despite this difference, the analysis has shown that in respect both of its theme and of the manner in which it is developed "The Nose", which Karlinsky has described as "the most authentically surrealistic of Gogol's works" and "the most logic-defying piece of writing in Russian literature to this day",[37] is by no means so different from its predecessors as appearances would suggest. Transferring the scene of the events to St. Petersburg, which even in *Evenings* he had associated with the phenomenon of "heat",[38] Gogol merely converts the Russian capital with the aid of familiar symbols and allusive devices into the same kind of female-dominated realm as Dikan'ka and Mirgorod and makes it the battleground on which the same allegorical war is fought between the sexes. The only significant difference, as stated, is the more violent intrusion of the symbolic logic into the logic of normal experience. Forsaking the motivational device of dream that he had used in the first complete redaction, as in the concluding scene of "Shpon'ka", Gogol here "exposes" his symbols (to borrow a term from the Formalist critics) to an extent which has no parallel in his other works. Moving them into the foreground of the narrative, he more insistently invites us to decipher their meaning, impelling us to abandon our conventional notions of logical relationships[39] and to look instead for relationships that hinge on entirely different logical premises. In this sense the story that is traditionally regarded as his most impenetrable and perplexing work is paradoxically the most revealing introduction to his fictional universe.

FOOTNOTES TO CHAPTER IV

1.   N. I. Oulianoff, "Arabesque or Apocalypse? On the Fundamental Idea of Gogol's Story *The Nose*", *Canadian Slavic Studies*, vol. 1, 1967, pp. 159-60.
2.   See his letter of 28 September 1833 to M. P. Pogodin (X, 277).
3.   See Erlich, p. 84.
4.   H. E. Bowman, "The Nose", *The Slavonic and East European Review*, vol. 31, 1952, p. 209.
5.   Ibid., p. 210.
6.   See Gukovsky, pp. 280-95.
7.   See Oulianoff, pp. 158-71.
8.   See Yermakov, pp. 167-216.
9.   Belyy, p. 79.
10. See *PSS*, p. 684.
11. See Yermakov, pp. 108-12.

12. References to "The Nose", "The Overcoat" and "The Carriage", as well as to the other "Petersburg tales", are all to volume 3 of *PSS* and are entered hereafter in the text by page number only.

13. See the narrator's earlier reference to Riga and Kamchatka as marking Russia's boundaries (53).

14. St. Petersburg is not actually mentioned in Sobakevich's diatribe, but in an earlier version of the chapter the link with the capital was explicitly established (see VI, 747).

15. The cosmopolitan, "non-indigenous" character of St. Petersburg is evoked by such details as the references to the carriage imported from Paris and the turnip- and radish-seeds from London which the narrator incorporates in the list of items to be advertised in the newspaper (59-60).

16. The reference to Kovalyov's acquisition of his new rank in the Caucasus, which was notorious for its corrupt administration, is perhaps relevant to this point, for corruption and cheating can be counted among the vices which are emblematic in Gogol's works of the masculine mentality (cf. the various swindles of Chichikov, the cheating of Nozdryov at draughts (VI, 84-5), and Sobakevich's insertion of a female in his list of dead serfs (VI, 137)).

17. See the nose's announcement to Kovalyov in the cathedral: "I am an independent person, and there can be no close relations between us" (56).

18. See, for example, the comparison of Sobakevich's house to the type "which is built in Russia for military settlements" (VI, 93) and the portraits of the Greek generals and Bagration on the walls of his sitting-room (VI, 95).

19. See A. G. Preobrazhensky, *Etimologicheskiy slovar' russkogo yazyka*, vol. 1 (Moscow, 1959), p. 116.

20. The fact that the children comprise only a junior "barber" seems to be implied in Ivan Yakovlevich's offer to shave the inspector "twice or *even* three times" a week. In other words, the third shave, like the third "barber", is rather in the nature of an afterthought.

21. See *GDS*, pp. 36-7. The dialogue, begun by Chichikov, is as follows:

"— . . . я вовсе не охотник играть.

— Отчего же не охотник? . . .

— Потому что не охотник"(VI, 81).

22. See the references to the "sugary sweetness" of Manilov's eyes (VI, 16, 25) and to the expression on his face which is "not only sweet, but sickly, like the medicine which a clever society doctor has sweetened unmercifully in the belief that it will please his patient" (VI, 29).

23. An echo of the two motifs may perhaps be detected in Kovalyov's reference to the women who sell "peeled oranges" on the Voskresensky Bridge (56). The detail conceivably conveys the same point in relation to the women of the capital as the "boiling" of fruit in the portrait of Shpon'ka's aunt.

24. Functioning as an expression of the symbolic theme of emasculation, the motif of sleep or physical inactivity is perceptible in many seemingly random details that Gogol includes in "The Nose". The most notable examples are to be found in the catalogue of objects due to be advertised by the people whom Kovalyov meets in the newspaper office: a carriage imported from Paris which, though twenty years old, is "little worn"; a seventeen-year-old horse which is still "young and spirited"; and a number of "boot-soles" which, though old, are evidently still fit for use (59-60). In each case the discrepancy between condition and age implies the inactivity of the owners. Equally noteworthy is Kovalyov's contention that staff-officers, when visiting the theatre, should have seats "in the stalls (*v kreslakh* – literally "in armchairs") (62).

25. It may perhaps be inferred that the selection of this location, like that of the Kazan Cathedral earlier, was prompted by "military" considerations − by the allusion that it introduces to Field Marshall Prince G. A. Potyomkin-Tavricheskiy, after whom the garden was named and who had already made a personal appearance in Gogol's fiction, as will be seen in the next chapter. The account of the nose's flight thus ends, as it begins, with an allusion to a prominent Russian "warrior".

26. Cf. the statement in the first complete redaction of the tale that Kovalyov, having failed to reattach the nose, "became so thin and emaciated in the course of a month that he was more like a corpse than a human being" (399).

27. Yermakov, p. 187. Cf. Peter C. Spycher, "N. V. Gogol's 'The Nose': a Satirical Comic Fantasy Born of an Impotence Complex", *The Slavic and East European Journal*, vol. 7, 1963, p. 370.

28. See the reference to the barber's "perpetually stinking hands" (51) and the similarity to the "stinking" subconscious of Chichikov in the form of the malodorous Petrushka (VI, 20) (see *GDS*, p. 53).

29. Cf. the description of Storchenko's mother in "Shpon'ka" as "a regular coffee-pot in a cap" (I, 298).

30. See supra, p. 30.

31. See in this connection V. I. Yeremina's comments on the distinction between the two traditions (the Russian and the Ukrainian) on which Gogol appears to draw in his portrayal of the mermaid (*Russkaya literatura i fol'klor (pervaya polovina XIX v.)* (Leningrad, 1976), p. 257).

32. It may again be noted that on his arrival at Korobochka's estate Chichikov is immediately subjected to blows from both these symbolic weapons − first to a lashing by her symbolic rain (VI, 41), then to the heat of her enormous quilts (VI, 47).

33. This interpretation of the fish is perhaps indirectly supported by the image of the fisherman that is evoked in the portrait of Shpon'ka's aunt (see supra, p. 18).

34. In the initial draft of the story it was situated on Voznesensky *Street* (380).

35. Yermakov, p. 203.

36. See the barber's reaction on being prevented from touching the nose: "Ivan Yakovlevich even let his hands drop; he was struck dumb and became more confused than he had ever been before" (74).

37. Karlinsky, pp. 123, 129.

38. See the description of the city in "Christmas Eve" as "bathed in light" (*ves' v ogne* − literally "all in fire") (I, 232).

39. Cf. the comment of Viktor Vinogradov: "The customary associations and combinations of words and facts are deliberately destroyed" (V. V. Vinogradov, *Evolyutsiya russkogo naturalizma. Gogol' i Dostoyevsky* (Leningrad, 1929), p. 49).

V

"THE OVERCOAT"

The Overcoat" is probably the best known and most frequently discussed short story in Russian literature. It was first published in 1842 and was thus the last of Gogol's "Petersburg tales" to make its appearance. According to his contemporary and associate P. V. Annenkov, however, the initial conception of the work dates from the mid-thirties. Hence, we may assume, its position in the middle of the cycle. But rather more important is Annenkov's recollection of the jolt that triggered off the conception — the oft-quoted account of the anecdote that was told in Gogol's presence about a poor clerk who was a passionate hunter and who eventually succeeded by dint of remarkable self-discipline and industry in saving enough money to purchase an expensive hunting-gun. His joy was short-lived. On his first expedition with the gun it was irretrievably lost, swept into the water by reeds while his attention was diverted. "The clerk returned home," Annenkov continues, "took to his bed and stayed there: he caught a fever. He was restored to life only by the subscription of his friends, who learned of the incident and bought him a new gun, but he could never recall the occurrence without turning deathly pale ... The anecdote, which was based on a true incident, made everyone laugh except Gogol, who listened to it thoughtfully and lowered his head."[1]

Every student of Russian literature is familiar with this anecdote, and repetition would seem to be unnecessary. But regarding it in the light of the recurrent symbols that have been identified in this study, we can now appreciate why it made such a deep impression on Gogol. On hearing this tale of a hunter losing his highly valued gun in a pool of water, he must have felt that he was listening to one of his own symbolic plots, to a variation of his own tale about the major who loses his highly valued nose in the river Neva. He must have been reminded of his own "hunters" Afanasy Ivanovich and Ivan Nikiforovich who through neglect and disrepair had also lost their guns. If we accept, therefore, Annenkov's assertion that "The Overcoat" was inspired by the anecdote, there is clearly a *prima facie* case for approaching the story with the presupposition that it presents yet another variation of the familiar symbolic theme developed in the familiar narrative style. To do so, of course, is to take issue at once with preceding interpretations of the work and to invite a scathing response, but once more it is hoped to show that the approach offers answers to the familiar problems that have traditionally taxed the minds of critics — the problems of interpreting seemingly pointless details, reconciling ostensibly conflicting elements and relating the narrator's apparent digressions to the central theme. Let us, then, consider the intrinsic evidence, beginning with the hero's portrait.

The details of the portrait convey vividly Akaky Akakiyevich's kinship with his emasculated predecessors in Gogol's fiction. After reading, for example, the story of Major Kovalyov, we can hardly regard as coincidence the absence of any reference to his nose. The silence on this subject, it may be noted, distinguishes the final version of the portrait from the first draft, in which the nose was described at some length. It was described as "not very remarkable, blunt and rather similar to the cakes called buns (*pyshkami*) which are made by the (female) cooks (*kukharki*) of St. Petersburg" (448). In this version, therefore, the nose of Akaky Akakiyevich, like that of Kovalyov, shows signs of having been baked by a female cook, meriting comparison on emerging from its ordeal to a particular kind of cake, the name of which (*pyshka*) significantly has the figurative meaning "a plump woman". Moreover, it was also indicated in the first draft that the hero "even shaved without a mirror" (447), presumably because the *pyshka* was so flat that there was little risk of catching it with the razor. In the final version, however, Gogol opted, as stated, for total silence, evidently regarding it as a more effective means of conveying the insignificance of the organ.

Other details in the portrait which likewise acquire important meaning in the light of the earlier analyses are the weakness of the hero's sight, which may similarly be interpreted, like the inspector's identical affliction in "The Nose", as signifying a kind of anaesthetization of the senses, a deadening of the sensual acuteness that distinguishes such "nosey" hunters as Nozdryov; the "small bald patch" on the top of his head, the implication of which is suggested by the contrast with the "thick black hair" that seems to cover Nozdryov's entire body (VI, 64, 83); his pock-marked features, which may be regarded in the light of later details as additional testimony to the rigours of the "baking" process; and the "haemorrhoidal" hue of his complexion, which may be taken to allude not simply to the sedentary nature of his occupation but, more basically, to the lack of masculine vitality that condemns him to be a "perpetual Titular Counsellor". And as in the portrait of Shpon'ka, this lack of vitality and consequent detachment from the normal processes of life are reflected in a remarkably inhibited mode of speech.[2]

Once more, however, it is the hero's name that merits particular attention. Although Driessen and, more recently, J. Schillinger have argued with some force that Gogol probably had in mind the sixth-century St. Acacius of Sinai,[3] the entire portrait of the clerk before his metamorphosis into vengeful ghost and Gogol's already attested practice of making effective use of names of Greek derivation suggest that the name was chosen principally because of the expressiveness of its Greek root — the noun *akakia* which means "guilelessness, innocence, simplicity". The portrait would suggest, in other words, that the name was intended to allude to the attitude of emphatically "unmasculine" submissiveness which is the hero's most prominent character trait. But again it is important to note that, like the surname of the hero of "Shpon'ka", the name is borne not only by the hero. As significant as the name itself and the repressed status that it implies is its reappearance in the patronymic, which suggests, of course, that his father had enjoyed the same status, and this conclusion in its turn prompts the further conjecture that the latter's premature death[4] is thereby explained, that like the husbands of Korobochka and Podtochina he has been not only emasculated but even exterminated. And if this interpretation is correct, we can readily appreciate the force of the narrator's statement that to give the hero a name other than Akaky "was quite out of the question" (143). As in "Shpon'ka", the fate of the father predetermines the fate of the son or, as the hero's mother puts it at his christening: "His father was Akaky, so let his son be Akaky" (142). The relevance of these implications to the surname soon becomes apparent.

In the second redaction of the tale Gogol chose a surname which similarly expressed the idea of submissiveness — Tishkevich (451), which is derived from the adjective *tikhiy* ("quiet") and may likewise be related to the motif of "peace". In the final version, however, he replaced it with a surname that seems to imply the cause of this psychological condition rather than the condition itself, i.e. with a surname which implicitly explains the Christian name. The name Bashmachkin is derived from the diminutive form of the masculine noun *bashmak* ("shoe"),[5] and it is significant for two reasons: unlike the earlier variant Bashmakov, it has the adjectival suffix *-in* which is normally attached to derivatives of feminine nouns, and the noun *bashmak* is reserved in the tale exclusively for female footwear. Indeed, Gogol is at pains to emphasize that the feet of the male Bashmachkins are clad in *sapogi* ("boots") and, in general, establishes in the course of the story a no less close association between *sapogi* and the feet of males than between *bashmaki* and the feet of females. In combination with the suffix these associations would seem to imply the obviously important point that the name Bashmachkin comes from the female side of the family, i.e. that the family surname, which is normally taken from the male, and the masculine authority that it connotes have been usurped by the family's females.

The question, however, remains: why did Gogol take the name specifically from female footwear? The answer is indirectly suggested by the earlier works in which he had used the related symbol *cherevik*, which is the Ukrainian word for a type of high-heeled leather boot worn by women. Thus in "Christmas Eve", we note, the imperious Oksana, who is described at one point as "standing like an empress" (I, 221), flaunts her power over the blacksmith Vakula by insisting that he acquire for her not simply a pair of *chereviki*, but the *chereviki* of the Empress Catherine herself. "Get me the Empress's *chereviki*, blacksmith," she cries, "and I will marry you" (I, 216). In other words, she is prepared to contemplate marriage only when equipped with these symbols of the authority of an empress who has usurped her husband's throne. Here *chereviki* are associated with female power, and this association plainly highlights the signif-

icance in "The Sorochintsy Fair" of the name of Solopy Cherevik, who undergoes such torment at the hands of the shrewish Khivrya. In addition, it provides
support for our interpretation of the statement in "Shpon'ka" in which the
noun *bashmak* is encountered for the first time performing an apparently similar
symbolic role — namely, Masha's reply to Shpon'ka's remark about the flies in
summer, where the symbol alludes, we have suggested, to the power over
Storchenko of his mother, to his reduction to the status of a swotted fly.
Considered in relation to the name Bashmachkin, these earlier references and
allusions to female footwear point to a single conclusion — that in each case
Gogol had in mind a particular Russian expression involving the noun *bashmak*
which relates precisely to the male's submission to female authority: *byt' pod
bashmakom u zheny*, which means "to be henpecked" (literally "to be under the
shoe of one's wife"). And if this hypothesis is correct, it means, of course, that
the name Bashmachkin is not only derived from the family's females but was
chosen specifically to allude to female repression of the male.

Although, however, the hypothesis may seem plausible when considered in
relation to the position of the hero's father, its relevance to the apparently
unmarried, though "fly-like",[6] hero may well seem a little questionable, for if
there is no wife, how can there be a repressive uxorial shoe? But is the hero
unmarried, as appearances would seem to suggest? It is in this connection that
we need to consider the most mystifying of the narrator's remarks in the context
of his comments on the hero's name — the statement in which he includes
"even" the hero's brother-in-law (*shurin*) in the list of male Bashmachkins who
allegedly "wore boots, re-soling them only two or three times a year" (142).
Given the female domination of the male Bashmachkins and the significance of
the epithet "haemorrhoidal" in the portrait of the hero, the implications of the
concluding phrase can hardly be doubted. Like the discrepancy between the age
and condition of the "boot-soles" that are advertised in "The Nose", the
infrequent need to re-sole the boots can only be taken to allude to the defective
vitality of those who wear them. But what are we to make of the noun *shurin*
which means specifically "a wife's brother" and thus implicitly attributes the
hero with a wife? Only one critic has thus far shown a due awareness of this
problem — Richard Peace, who links the allusion with the reference on the
following page to the hero's seventy-year-old landlady (*khozyayka*) who is
apparently suspected by his colleagues of wishing to marry him. Having established the link, however, Peace does little more than suggest the presence of a
"latent sexual motif" and ultimately resigns himself to identifying merely one
more Gogolian puzzle and absurdity.[7] Yet the link does provide an answer to
the puzzle and offers another vivid illustration of the tremendous demands that
Gogol makes on his readers' powers of inference. The landlady, we note, is not
only suspected of wishing to marry the hero; she is also attributed by rumour
with the habit of beating him (143). In addition, our attention is later drawn to
her *bashmaki* (162) and she is a *khozyayka* — a term which means not only

"landlady" but also "mistress" or "female superior". In other words, the "landlady" is indirectly credited with the authority and capacity for violence which are the hallmarks of a typical Gogolian wife, and even the fact that she is some twenty years older than the hero does not weaken the argument that she is indeed his wife, for the difference of age merly enhances her authoritative status.

It may be objected, of course, that if the "landlady" were already the hero's wife, his colleagues could hardly be unaware of it. But is it really so inconceivable, given his remarkable "quietness" and detachment from people, that he has simply failed to disclose the fact? Indeed, bearing in mind the usual reasons for male "quietness" in Gogol's works, may we not conclude that his silence on this, as on every other subject, is one of the clearest indications that he is, in fact, a married man? He is silent, we may deduce, because he has been crushed beneath his mistress's *bashmak*, because he has forfeited in marriage, like his father, whatever vestige of masculine authority he may once have possessed. The entire life of Akaky Akakiyevich has been spent under a female shoe — first that of his mother, then that of his wife; hence the psychological condition reflected in the details of his portrait.

The conclusion, therefore, is not only that the "landlady" is the wife whose existence is conveyed by the reference to the hero's brother-in-law, but also that she is a typical Gogolian wife whose authority is signified not by a "terrible masculine hand" but rather by her *bashmaki* and by the name Bashmachkina which alludes to them. For if her brother is named Bashmachkin, as the narrator's reference to him suggests, we must conclude that her name was Bashmachkina even before she received it from the hero as a consequence of their marriage. The significance of the point may be inferred from the implications of the name as they have been interpreted. Far from representing an implausible coincidence, the identity of her maiden name with the hero's surname merely strengthens the argument that it is less a surname than a symbol, a symbol of female power which alludes to the nature of the sexual relationship that prevails not only in the family of the hero. The inclusion of the "landlady's" brother in the list of male Bashmachkins is the first hint that Gogol provides in the story that the males of the hero's family are not the only victims of *bashmaki*, that every male in the capital, in fact, has suffered or is doomed to suffer a similar fate. This would explain why surnames are explicitly bestowed in the tale only on the hero's family and brother-in-law. Every other male, it is implied, is similarly a Bashmachkin and every female a Bashmachkina, a usurper of masculine authority. The story as it unfolds confirms this conclusion. The portraits of the other males in the story, together with numerous combinations of details which critics have tended to regard as digressions, reinforce the contention that Gogol's theme here, as in "The Nose", is the usurpation of masculine authority by the female, and the consequent emasculation of the male, not simply in the experience of his hero, but in all reaches of society in Russia's capital city and thus, implicitly, in Russian society as a whole. Hence the agitation in the opening paragraph of the tale of the provincial police-captain who states that his name, the symbol of his authority, is "being taken in vain" and that "the institutions of the state are being destroyed" (141). In "The Overcoat" the city of Peter the Great is again portrayed as a realm in which power has fallen into female hands.

Like so many of the most revealing statements in Gogol's works, the most important allusion to the act of usurpation is simply mentioned by the narrator in passing, as if its significance were minimal — namely, the "everlasting anecdote", which the hero's young colleagues are given to recounting, about "the commanding officer who was told that the tail had been cut off the horse on Falconet's monument" (146). The idea of emasculation, of course, is immediately suggested, and the suspicion that the allusion is less to the emasculation of the horse than to that of its rider is reinforced by the more equivocal version of the sentence in the first draft of the story, which stated that "the tail had been cut off the statue of Peter" (447). Moreover, an additional basis for this suspicion is provided by two episodes in Gogol's earlier works in which males are actually converted into horses by the females who attack them — the episode in "The Sorochintsy Fair" in which Solopy is discovered prostrate on the road with his wife Khivrya on his back (I, 128-9),[8] and the battle for supremacy in "Viy" in which Khoma Brut and the witch ride one another (II, 185-8).[9] In these episodes the notion of riding and the image of the horse are clearly identified as metaphors respectively of victory and defeat in sexual conflict. The confusion, therefore, of Peter with his horse, combined with the reference to the horse's docked tail, not only identifies him as another defeated male, but suggests that the function of the "anecdote" is to introduce the idea of the usurpation of male authority in the capital by evoking the notion of the emasculation of the Emperor who founded the city. At the same time, however, there are grounds for believing that the image of the emasculated Peter contains a more precise allusion, an allusion to a particular female usurper, and that in choosing this particular "anecdote" Gogol was mindful of the curious change that took place in the history of the Russian monarchy after Peter's death — namely, the occupation of the throne for sixty-six of the next seventy-one years by females, who had never before ruled Russia except in periods of regency. He could well have had in mind the popular saying that expressed the eighteenth-century peasant's reaction to this development: "Grain does not grow because the female sex controls the realm" (*khleb ne roditsya potomu, chto zhenskiy pol tsarstvom vladeyet*).[10]

It is in this connection that we need to recall once more Oksana's insistence in "Christmas Eve" on acquiring the *chereviki* of the usurper Catherine II and, more generally, Gogol's intriguing preference for setting the action of his tales of sexual conflict in *Evenings* in the years of Catherine's reign. Particularly noteworthy are the short descriptions in the volume of Catherine and her court. Thus when Vakula is led into the court in "Christmas Eve", he is struck at once by the profusion of females and, above all, by their attire. He "did not know," we read, "which way to look for the number of ladies who walked in wearing satin dresses with long trains (*khvostami*)" (I, 236). The significance of the statement lies not only in the allusion to female domination of the court, but also in the fact that the primary meaning of *khvost* is not "train" but "tail" and thus suggests the possibility of another expressive *double entendre* which associates the ladies of Catherine's court, like the witches who have been identified as the precursors of Gogol's masculinized females, with the devil.[11] Considered, there-fore, in the light of this statement, the brief reference in "The Lost Letter" (*Propavshaya gramota*) to Catherine sitting on her throne "in red boots (*sapo-gakh*)" (I, 191) may be seen to be highly revealing. Not only is she wearing boots, which may again allude to the idea of oppression, but they are in the devil's colour and they are *sapogi*, the boots of a male. Once more the idea of allegiance to the devil is combined with that of usurping the male's position. In addition to presiding over a coven of witches, Catherine is herself exposed as a witch and, as such, as an oppressor of males. The confirmation is the brief portrait in "Christmas Eve" of her Field Marshall and lover, the unfortunate Potyomkin, who is cast here in the same symbolic role as the later "warrior" Kutuzov in "The Nose" and chapter 3 of *Dead Souls* — the role of vanquished male. His hair, we are told, "was ruffled" (like that of Vasilisa Kashporovna's miller) and he "squinted a little in one eye" (I, 235), thus displaying his affinity with the "weak-sighted" Akaky Akakiyevich and the "short-sighted", henpecked inspector in "The Nose". And if we recall again the particular associations of the term "Cossack", we may now understand why Catherine in "Christmas Eve" has inflicted on the Zaporozhians who come to plead with her the many misfortunes that defy their comprehension. Indeed, she herself reveals the cause when she remarks to them: "I have heard that in the Sech' men never get married" (I, 238). The only males, it seems, who merit her favour are those who have submitted to female control. Hence her very different attitude to Vakula, who not only thirsts for marriage but aspires to reward his bride-to-be with the symbolic boots which predetermine his fate.

Finally, in addition to these illuminating details from the folkish stories of *Evenings*, we might also recall the implications of Peter III's portrait on the wall of Pul'kheriya Ivanovna's "little house" in "Old-World Landowners" and a remark by the narrator of "Shpon'ka" on the gesture with which Storchenko's mother registers her contempt for her son's neglect of the estate: "The old lady heaved a sigh, and an observer would have heard in that sigh the sigh of a past age, of the eighteenth century" (I, 304). Can we doubt that the sigh reflects her nostalgia for the age of Catherine, for an age in which the female ruled supreme and males like her son were kept firmly in their place?

What, then, it will be asked, is the relevance of all these references and allusions to Catherine to "The Overcoat" and the anecdote about Peter's statue? They are relevant, one might argue, in three senses. First of all, they testify that

Gogol was fully disposed to make use of Russia's rulers as symbolic figures wholly involved in the sexual warfare that lies at the centre of his tales. Indirectly, therefore, they render more plausible the contention that the emasculation of Peter's statue is significantly related to the theme of "The Overcoat". Secondly, the representation of Catherine as a figure antagonistic to males and of her reign as a period in which the female was omnipotent reinforces the suggestion that the emasculation of the statue was connected in Gogol's mind with the female domination of the Russian throne after Peter's death. And, finally, the episodes and details that have been referred to provide a clue to the meaning of one of the most intriguing statements in the tale — the statement that the Important Personage, on succumbing to a feeling of remorse after his savage treatment of the hero, set off to see "a certain lady of his acquaintance, Karolina Ivanovna, a lady, it seems, of German extraction" (171).

The immediate assumption, of course, is that the lady is his mistress, and so, it appears, she is, but there is good reason to suspect that the term "mistress" is again appropriate here in the sense of *khozyayka*. For if this female, who is never mentioned again in the tale, is simply a paramour, why does Gogol not simply say so instead of giving her a name and even indicating her national origins? The answer that suggests itself is that these two seemingly superfluous pieces of information were meant to identify her as something else. Once more, therefore, we must turn to a name for the resolution of a mystery. In the first redaction of the epilogue the lady was given a different name — Nastas'ya Karlovna, which is related, of course, to the name in the final version by the fact that the name Karl which appears in the patronymic is the source of the Christian name Karolina. The important point, however, is that it is also the source of the Russian word for "king" (*korol'*). Both Karlovna and Karolina, in short, endow the lady with the aura of royalty, the former suggesting "the daughter of a king" and the latter "a queen" (*koroleva*) or "empress". And if the function of the names is indeed to convey these ideas, Gogol's reasons for preferring the Christian name are not difficult to deduce, for in combination with the suffix *-ina* the expressive root bears a striking resemblance to the name "(Ye)katerina" ("Catherine"). Moreover, only if we accept that "Karolina" is Gogol's mask of "Catherine" does the reference to her German extraction make any significant sense, for Catherine was herself, of course, a German princess before her marriage to Peter III — a fact of which Gogol reminds us in "Christmas Eve" by noting Vakula's assumption that the copper doorhandles in Catherine's palace have been made by "German blacksmiths" (I, 235). And it might also be observed that the word "German", as Gogol uses it in "Christmas Eve", seems to confirm Catherine's status in his works as witch. Not only is Vakula transported to her citadel, St. Petersburg, by the devil, but on the second page of the story the devil is compared to "a German" (I, 202) and is later addressed as "you damned German!" by Vakula (I, 225). Even if we make due allowance for the traditional Russian antipathy to Germans, the choice of word in both cases seems rather curious unless we take it as a forward-pointing allusion designed to associate with the devil the "German" Catherine who appears later.

The conclusion, therefore, to which these various considerations point is that in combination with the emphatically Russian patronymic Ivanovna the name Karolina alludes to the German princess with the notorious appetite for males who usurped her husband's throne to become the Russian Empress Catherine II — to the Empress who is obliquely portrayed in "Christmas Eve" as a witch in the devil's service and associated on two subsequent occasions with oppression of the male. As the most illustrious and imposing of the female sovereigns who acceded to the throne of Peter the Great, Catherine, it is suggested, is introduced into "The Overcoat" in her new deceptive guise as the central symbol of "diabolical" female power, as the female usurper *par excellence*, and the dominant symbol of her triumph is the emasculation of Peter's statue — a statue, we might recall, that was erected at her behest. Indeed, the inscription at the foot of the statue — *Petro primo Catharina secunda* — may conceivably have suggested to Gogol the symbolic relationship between the "great" Emperor and the "great" Empress that seems to lie at the basis of the tale, serving, like the inclusion of the hero's brother-in-law in the list of Bashmachkins, as a means of conveying a transition from male to female power which, far from being confined to the hero's family, has been effected throughout Petersburg society. Complementing the allusion to Peter with the allusion to Catherine, Gogol provides, as it were, an explanatory backcloth to the events of his story, implicitly relating to Catherine's *coup d'état* the female *coups* that have taken place in the households of his principal characters — most notably in that of the hero and in that of the tailor Petrovich, who significantly refers to his wife as "the German woman". The effect of the *coup*, it is implied, has been to transform the entire female population into Bashmachkinas, into "the cooks of St. Petersburg", versed in the special skill of reducing masculine noses to the condition of *pyshki*. Returning, therefore, to our point of departure, we may deduce from the narrator's disclosures that the Important Personage is "a good husband" and that his wife is "not in the least ugly" (171) that his intended visit to Karolina Ivanovna is by no means a call on a paramour, but rather a direct consequence of the softening of his attitude to the hero. As a servant of the Teutonic oppressor of males, he must account to her in person for any relaxation of the Teutonic discipline that she imposes.

In the light of this background it is now possible to determine the symbolic function in the tale of the Teutonic innovation which had such an immense impact on post-Petrine Russian society — the Table of Ranks, which is represented as the Empress's most potent instrument of emasculation. Again the symbolic idea of the "box" is evoked. Like the little pens and "boxes" in the greater "box" of the "boxy" Korobochka's estate, the various ranks in the Table seem to comprise a hierarchy of cells or "boxes" in which the vitality of the male is "sapped" with Teutonic efficiency. This explains why the distorting effects of rank on the personality receive almost as much emphasis in the portrait of the Important Personage, who sits in one of the highest "boxes", as in that of the hero, who sits in the ninth. "Compassion," we read, "was not unknown to him; his heart was open to many kindly impulses, though his rank often prevented them from being shown" (171). The higher the "box", of course, the more privileged the occupant's position and the greater his authority, but it is still a delegated authority wielded over the occupants of the lower "boxes" on behalf of the higher female authority. Hence the narrator's statement, which otherwise seems distinctly pointless, that despite the recent promotion of the Important Personage, "his position even now was not considered important compared with others of still greater importance" (164), and it is in this sense that Peace is right in asserting that the Important Personage, no less than the hero, is a "copier of words".[12]

The only important difference, in short, between the Important Personage and the hero is that the former occupies a higher "box" which imposes a different function. No less than the humble Titular Counsellor, who responds with total perplexity to the slight variation of his responsibilities suggested by a "kindly director" (144-5),[13] the nameless general is reduced to the condition of an automaton completely identified with the function to which his "box" condemns him. Initially he too, like Akaky Akakiyevich, is totally disorientated by the wider responsibilities that come with his promotion (165), though unlike the hero, of course, he eventually succeeds in adjusting to his new situation. And equally significant is the nature of his function: namely, to administer *raspekaniya* — a term which we take to mean "reprimands", but which literally means "comprehensive bakings".[14] As the hero emerges from the Important Personage's office, we read: "Never before in his life had he been so soundly reprimanded (*raspechen*) by a general . . .," and appropriately the sequel to the "baking" process is the "fever" (*goryachka*, derived from the verb *goret'* ("to burn")) which lays him low (167). It is inconceivable that these words were chosen at random. Once more, we must conclude, *double entendres* are used to introduce the motif that Gogol appears to reserve exclusively to signify *female* violence against the male — a motif which indirectly confirms the Important Personage's ancillary status, exposing him as a "tool" of the Teutonic sovereign who presides over "the cooks of St. Petersburg" and revealing perhaps the essential point of the narrator's observation: "In Holy Russia everything is infected with imitation; everyone apes and mimics his superior" (145). The Important Personage, it may be noted, is not the first official in Gogol's fiction to ape the manner of the German Empress. Ever since he had escorted Catherine on a tour of the Crimea, the headman (*golova*) in "A May Night", we are told, had been prone to "shoot hawk-like glances from under his brows" (I, 161). The Important Personage's *raspekaniya*, we may deduce, have been similarly inspired and thus strengthen the argument that his position, like that of the hero, is essentially that of a willless marionette performing mechanically its function in a uniform, female-dominated government machine. Hence the similar poverty of his conversation, which often consisted, in the narrator's phrase, "of certain monosyllabic sounds" (165), and the complete vacuity of his mind as he makes his way to the Empress's palace (172).

Differences of behaviour in the story, however, are not exclusively determined by the positions of "boxes" in the hierarchy. Another important determinant, it seems, is the duration of the inmate's confinement. The hero presents himself as the most comprehensively emasculated and puppet-like of the female sovereign's vassals not only because of the lowly position of his "box", but also because he has spent the longest time in it. "No one could remember," the narrator remarks, "when he entered the department or who appointed him" (143). As a result his prison, i.e. his role as functionary, has uniquely engulfed his entire existence, endowing it with that emblematic "peaceful" (*mirnaya*) quality (146) which is Gogol's most conclusive indicator of the affliction reflected in every detail of the clerk's portrait. The narrator observes: "It would hardly be possible to find a man who so lived in his work . . . Whatever Akaky Akakiyevich looked at, he saw inscribed on everything his own clear, evenly written lines . . ." (144-5). At home in his apartment, therefore, even the pleasures of eating are replaced by the pleasure of copying which has become a substitute for the gratification of his atrophied senses.[15] The lines of his writing have become the bars of a prison, resembling in their symbolic force Korobochka's "striped wall-paper" and the "striped petticoats" with which, as we have noted, Pul'kheriya Ivanovna vainly strives to prevent her serf girls from becoming pregnant, i.e. from asserting their vitality. Capable only of copying the words of others, he seems powerless to generate an independent thought.

The state of mind, however, of the hero's young colleagues in the department is notably different, as the narrator reveals in such passages as the following:

> Not once in his life had he paid any attention to the daily happenings in the street at which, as we all know, his colleagues (*brat*), the young clerks, always stare, extending the sharpness of their lively gaze (*boykogo vzglyada*) so far as to notice anyone on the other side of the pavement with a ripped off trouser strap hanging down — a sight which always brings a sly grin to their faces (145).

Once more Gogol enlists here, as in "Old-World Landowners" and chapter 6 of *Dead Souls* (the portrait of Plyushkin)[16] the symbolism of age to convey by contrast the dehumanization of his hero. Just as the portrait of the aged Plyushkin is prefaced with the narrator's reminiscences of his youth, so the portrait of the elderly, emasculated Akaky Akakiyevich is offset by the references to his youthful colleagues, whose senses, as their sight attests, are not only sharp but characterized by the epithet *boykiy* which in *Dead Souls* is inseparably associated with the ebulliently masculine Nozdryov.[17] Hence the mirth with which they react to such evidence of emasculation as "a ripped off trouser strap hanging down" and the hero's undeviating preoccupation with his duties as vassal. It may be concluded, therefore, that the relationship between the hero and the young clerks is an essentially inimical relationship between the person-ifications of extreme and minimal degrees of emasculation and that the young clerks represent the positive pole of the contrast.

The importance of this point is considerable, for it highlights at once the misconception that underlies the usual formulation by critics of one of the major problems raised by the work — the problem posed by the celebrated "sentimental" passage in which the young clerks are charged with "inhumanity" and "savage brutality" (144) and which expresses a degree of compassion for the hero that seems sharply at variance with the otherwise uninhibited portrayal of his squalid existence. The conclusion to be drawn from the indicated interpreta-tion of the contrast is that the problem involves the reconciliation not of two conflicting attitudes to the hero and the young clerks expressed by the author but rather of the author's attitude and the contrasting attitude of the narrator, the latter of which (the compassionate attitude) is expressed directly, while the former, as always, is conveyed by symbol. In other words, we are confronted here once more with exactly the same kind of situation that we have encoun-tered in "Old-World Landowners", in which the symbolism, as we have seen, similarly contradicts the narrator's sympathetic attitude towards the heroine. Setting literal and symbolic levels of meaning in opposition to one another, Gogol again produces the paradox that with almost every word that he utters the narrator is unwittingly invalidating his own arguments and attitudes. On the literal level, as stated, the young clerks are branded with "inhumanity" and severely criticised for disturbing the hero in the execution of his duties. On the symbolic level, by contrast, their jibes and interference are ironically indicative of their profound "humanity", signifying not only their aversion to a mechanical marionette, but also their aspiration to restore him to life, to prise open the bars of his prison. And the same ironic interplay between contrasting levels of meaning is likewise perceptible in the description of the newly appointed young clerk through whom the narrator's sympathy for the hero is chiefly expressed, for the bond of sympathy that alienates him from the other young clerks can only be regarded, if our interpretation is correct, as an ironic indicator of his psychological kinship with the hero, of the "fraternal" affinity which prompts him to overhear in the hero's appeal for "peace" the words: "I am your brother" (145). His sympathy, in short, would seem to identify him as a young man whose youthful vitality, like that of the hero at the outset of his career, has already been "sapped" even before the transition to his "box" in the hierarchy. Yet not for nothing, we may assume, is the term *brat* (literally "brother") used also to denote the hero's "lively" colleagues. The implication is clearly that the emasculated automaton whom at present they mock is a mirror of the fate that lies before them. As inmates of the same "box", they too will succumb in time to the "heat" of *respekaniya* and of the other major instrument of the sovereign's authority — the St. Petersburg climate.

At first sight the imputation of this symbolic role to the capital's climate might well appear to place an intolerable strain on credulity, but perhaps a different view might be taken if, recalling the symbolism of "The Nose", we note the comparison of a blizzard to the work of a barber in the story that Gogol clearly had much in mind when creating "The Overcoat" — "Christmas Eve". Referring to Oksana's father Chub, the narrator observes: "At times a look of mawkish sweetness appeared on his face, though the blizzard had scraped his beard and moustache with snow more briskly than any barber who tyrannically seizes his victim by the nose" (I, 215). It is precisely the same tyrannical barber's role that the climate performs in "The Overcoat". The first indication of it is provided on the first page of the story by the causal connection which the narrator establishes between its rigours and the hero's "haemorrhoidal" complexion. Thereafter its function is progressively clarified, and again the context of the narrator's most explicit remarks on the subject is worthy of note, for they follow directly after his reference to the "various disasters which bestrew the path through life not only of Titular Counsellors, but even of Privy, Actual, Court and all other counsellors ..." (146-7). In other words, the sequence reinforces the impression that the climate is the source of the "disasters" which have befallen not only the hero but also the Important Personage. The "activity" of the climate is then described as follows:

> Between eight and nine o'clock in the morning, at precisely the hour when the streets are filled with officials going to their departments, it begins to administer such powerful and stinging flicks to all their noses indiscriminately that the poor fellows don't know where to put them. At this time, when even those in the highest posts have a pain in their brows from the frost and tears in their eyes, the poor Titular Counsellors are sometimes defenceless (147).

In addition, therefore, to clouding vision by bringing tears to the eyes, the frost is principally directed at the same object as the heat of Praskov'ya Osipovna's oven — at the nose of the male. Accordingly, the seemingly paradoxical use of the verb *propekat'* (ostensibly "to nip", in reality "to bake thoroughly") a few lines later to describe its effect on the hero's back and shoulders is not unduly surprising. The verb identifies the frost as a source of emasculating heat which affects the noses of "those in the highest posts" no less than that of the hero.

As the narrator indicates, however, the most grievous sufferings are endured by the Titular Counsellors and, above all, by the "perpetual Titular Counsellor". Appropriately, the most comprehensively emasculated official in the tale is the most "thoroughly baked", the most defenceless in the face of the capital's heat, and the symbol of his defences, of course, is his threadbare overcoat. Such is the pattern of imagery that links the image of the overcoat with the theme of emasculation, explaining the disparaging term by which the young clerks refer to it: *kapot* ("a woman's housecoat") (147). In effect, the overcoat, like its wearer, has itself been emasculated, and its condition is aptly mirrored in that of his trousers, boots, shirts and underwear, all of which are likewise in urgent need of repair or replacement (153).

The origins of the image, as we have noted, can be traced back to Shpon'ka's dream, in which the notion of a wife is associated with the kind of "woollen material" out of which frock-coats are made. And since Ivan Fyodorovich can only conceive of wives endowed with the dominating masculine attributes of his fearsome aunt, we may reasonably infer that such attributes are implicit in the image. Hence, perhaps, Rudyy Pan'ko's reference in the Foreword to *Evenings* to the "overall of fine cloth" for which the masculine sacristan of the Dikan'ka church, Foma Grigor'yevich, "paid almost six roubles a yard" (I, 104).[18] And we might again recall in this connection the motifs of "stripping" and "nakedness" (or "near-neakedness") which have been traced in the portraits of Storchenko, Afanasy Ivanovich, Ivan Nikiforovich, Ivan Yakovlevich (alias Kovalyov) and Chichikov, in whom these attributes are "sapped" by female adversaries. The association of "nakedness" with emasculation in these portraits would plainly seem to confirm that the image of the coat in Gogol's fiction is to be taken as a symbol of masculinity and, accordingly, that threadbare coats denote "threadbare" masculinity. Yet the important point is clearly that, despite its condition, Akaky Akakiyevich's coat is still an overcoat and therefore offers some "defence", however inadequate, against the assault of the "heat". It can only be regarded, in other words, as confirming by its very existence that his masculinity, however "threadbare" it may be and despite the accumulated evidence that appears to suggest the opposite, has still not been completely "sapped". And the same conclusion, of course, is prompted by his efforts to have it repaired, which can only be interpreted, if our assumptions are correct, as reflecting a desire for stronger "defences". The role of the tailor, therefore, to whom he turns is not difficult to determine.

Although Petrovich is not a civil servant, he is just as subject as Akaky Akakiyevich and the Important Personage to the heat inflicted by a "German woman". At the same time the forms that it assumes are somewhat different. It is noted, for example, that the stairs which lead to his apartment "were all soaked with water and slops (*pomoyami*) and saturated through and through with that smell of spirits which stings the eyes and is inseparable, as we all know, from the backstairs of Petersburg houses" (148). The implications of this "smell of spirits", which is significantly alleged to be a feature of every house in the capital, are most obviously disclosed by its effect on the eyes, which not only links it with the St. Petersburg climate, but also suggests the reason for the loss of one eye which links Petrovich with the two males in *Evenings* who perform duties for the Empress Catherine — the headman in "A May Night", whose tyrannical housekeeper, his sister-in-law (I, 161), is clearly a precursor of

Petrovich's "German woman", and Potyomkin in "Christmas Eve".[19] In addition, of course, we are reminded of the parallel image in "The Nose", in which Kovalyov is recommended to immerse his nose in "a jar of spirit". Implicitly explaining Petrovich's habitual drunkenness, the image of the spirit may be related directly, like the image of the climate, to Gogol's culinary imagery, to the metaphor of pickling and, above all, to the image of the heat which is generated by the "cooks of St. Petersburg", and as if to confirm the fact, Gogol immediately afterwards portrays the "German woman" vigorously engaged in the task of "cooking some fish". As "The Nose" (in this case the portrait of Ivan the servant) again suggests, the choice of dish is not coincidental, and it probably explains why the stairs are soaked in water as well as spirit. Frequent washings of his nose in "cold water" comprise, as we have seen, another course of treatment that is recommended to Kovalyov, and we may again recall that the masculine organ is initially propelled by Ivan Yakovlevich into the midst of the fish which inhabit the Neva. Moreover, it may be noted in *Evenings* that the misfortunes of the "grandfather" in "A Place Bewitched" culminate in the ordeal of a soaking in slops (*pomoi*) inflicted by a female (I, 315). Considered in the light of these details and of the indicated symbolism of the image of water neither the water on the stairs, we may conclude, nor the fish in the "German woman's" pan is mentioned without cause. While Kovalyov (in the guise of Ivan Yakovlevich) is reduced to a "newly baked loaf" by the "heat" of Podtochina (in the guise of Praskov'ya Osipovna), Petrovich is reduced to a "cooked fish" by the "heat" of his Teutonic spouse.[20] Hence the pock marks on his face, which relate him to the hero and reflect the rigours of his ordeal.

In addition to one eye, Petrovich, we are told, has also forfeited the meaningful Christian name "Grigory" that he shares with Storchenko. Ironically, it is stated that he lost the name and began to be called by his patronymic when he "acquired his freedom" (148), to which in the first draft of the tale Gogol added the words: "... got married and began to drink rather heavily on public holidays" (449).[21] At the same time, although he has lost one eye, his retention of the other, despite its weakness,[22] can only be taken to imply that his emasculation, like that of the hero, is still not complete, which would presumably explain his wife's continued activity in the kitchen. Support for this conclusion is provided not only by his unflattering references to his wife, which suggest that his resistance has not yet been broken,[23] but most obviously by the symbolism of his profession, which may be deduced from the indicated symbolic meaning of coats in Gogol's works, and, in particular, by his special expertise in the art of "repairing the trousers and coats of civil servants and others — naturally enough, when he was sober ..." (148). Not only, in other words, are Petrovich's own defences still resisting the "heat"; his entire purpose in life ("when he was sober") is to bolster the defences of others. Considered in relation to the allusions in the tale to Peter I and Catherine, this definition of his role, combined with the disclosure that "Petrovich loved to taunt Germans whenever the opportunity presented itself" (151), provides a basis for further speculations about his identity.

In the first draft of the story the tailor was given the Christian name Peter (449); in the final version he is "the son of Peter". Given the importance in the work of the reference to Falconet's statue, it is difficult to believe that these names were random choices, and the suspicion that a connection was intended is notably strengthened by the narrator's seemingly pointless remark in the first draft that he has no knowledge of whether Petrovich "was married to his third wife or his first" (449), for while the text provides no evidence to contradict the assumption that the "German woman" is his first wife in his incarnation as tailor, she may indeed be regarded as his third wife if he is meant to be a mask or double of the twice-married Emperor. Nor is his name the only evidence in the final version that supports this hypothesis, for it may be noted, in addition, that just as Peter is merged with the image of his horse, so equine allusions with presumably the same expressive force are introduced into the portrait of the tailor — for example, the verb *osadilsya*, which is used by his wife in the phrase *osadilsya sivukhoy* ("he has been pacified (literally "reined") by raw vodka"[24]) (149), and the reference to his "big toe" with its "misshapen nail as thick and strong as the shell of a tortoise" (149), which is conceivably intended to evoke the notion of a hoof. These details significantly reinforce the impression that the link which is forged between Petrovich's wife and Catherine (alias Karolina Ivanovna) by the references to their German origin is paralleled by a similar link between Petrovich and Peter. What, then, is the nature of this link? The answer would seem to be indicated by the substitution of "Petrovich" for "Peter", for the replacement of Christian name by patronymic would suggest that the initial intention of presenting the tailor as a mask of Peter was replaced by that of presenting him as Peter's "spiritual son", as a symbolic extension of the Emperor's personality; and if this is indeed his intended role, then we may perhaps assume that his wife plays a similar role in relation to the Empress Catherine. The conclusion of the hypothesis, in short, is that the allusively conveyed symbolic conflict between Russia's two greatest sovereigns which forms the explanatory backcloth to the events of the tale is linked directly with the hero by means of the dramatised conflict between Petrovich and his wife.

If this hypothesis, therefore, is correct, and if Petrovich's symbolic role in the fiction has been correctly defined, we can only conclude that despite the *coup d'état* and the allusion to the emasculation of Peter, the masculine spirit of the Emperor has not been completely destroyed, that it lives on in the figure of the symbolic tailor who repairs overcoats and trousers, communicating its own weakened, but still defiant, strength to the minority of the capital's males who have not irrevocably succumbed. Hence, perhaps, the simile in which Petrovich is compared to a "Turkish Pasha". Despite his mutilated body and the need to ply his trade surreptitiously without a signboard and from an inconspicuous side-street (156), he still merits comparison to a general of the nation which was the main adversary of the Empress Catherine — a general whose battles with the "German woman", to judge from the military symbol of his snuff-box, may have cost him his head,[25] but whose spirit has survived the onslaught.

While Peter, therefore, and all that he represents is rejected by Pushkin's clerk Yevgeny in *The Bronze Horseman* (*Mednyy vsadnik*), Akaky Akakiyevich is impelled by forces in his nature of which he is seemingly unconscious to turn to "the son of Peter" for urgently required assistance, and his appeal is duly granted. Significantly the words and actions of Petrovich during the negotiations, like the references earlier to the hero's young colleagues, repeatedly evoke the familiar image of the aggressive, misogynistic Nozdryov. We note, for example, the insertion of the emblematic *double entendre okhotnik* into the descriptive phrase applied to him *okhotnik zalamlivat' chert znayet kakiye tseny* (literally "a lover (-cum-hunter) of charging the devil only knows what prices") and the continuation of the hunting metaphor in the reference to his attempts to detect "what kind of bag (*dobychu*)" the hero has brought with him (149). The implication of the metaphor needs little comment. Supporting our interpretation of the tailor's role, it clearly explains his choice of term to express his scorn for the threadbare *kapot* — the gallicism *garderob*, which is reinvested with the meaning of its source (*garde-robe*) "a woman's apron or overall".

Like the hero's decision to visit Petrovich in the first place, his acceptance both of the tailor's uncompromising verdict that a new overcoat is needed and of the sacrifices that its acquisition entails points unambiguously to the possibility of his resurrection. Undeterred by the attempt on the street to subdue him with "a cap of lime" (152), he accedes to the tailor's demands, thereby registering his affirmative response to the offer to change him into a "new *man*". The very thought of the new coat, we observe, has an immediate "masculinizing" or reanimating effect on him, causing his heart, which "in general was very peaceful", to begin beating (155) and momentarily liberating the man from the functional automaton. A mistake almost creeps into his copying (155), and later, when the coat has been acquired, the consumption of food becomes a delight and domestic copying is promptly abandoned (158). His experience is the reverse of that which is undergone by Shpon'ka. Instead of seeing the threat of female power in the form of material for a masculine-gender frock-coat (*syurtuk*), he sees his new feminine-gender overcoat (*shinel'*) as the means of acquiring such power for himself, as the "wife" from whom he will obtain it. Unlike his actual wife (the *khozyayka*), the new "wife" will be a part of him. It is in this sense that we should understand the narrator's words: "From this time forth his existence seemed somehow to be more complete, as if he had married, as if another person were present with him, as if he were not alone but accompanied by a pleasing female companion who had agreed to complete life's journey together with him . . ." (154). And the narrator continues:

He became somehow more alive, more strong-willed even, like a man who has already determined and established his aim. Doubt, indecision, in short all signs of hesitation and uncertainty vanished automatically from his face and actions. At times a gleam appeared in his eyes, and the most bold and daring thoughts even flashed through his head: should he not really put marten on the collar? (154-5).

Here there is no comic bathos, as the concluding question would seem to suggest, for the image of the carnivorous marten alludes directly to the hero's incipient emancipation from his former self — from the category of Titular Counsellors "who cannot bite" (142) — and although the collar is ultimately made of cat fur, it is still "cat fur which at a distance could always be taken for marten" (155).

Despite the zeal with which Petrovich applies himself to the task, two whole weeks are required to complete the coat. The reason, in the narrator's words, is "the considerable amount of quilting (*stegan'ya*)"; in the author's words, it is "the considerable amount of whipping" (155). The *double entendre* conveys the "German woman's" ferocious interventions. But at last the tailor proudly unfurls the completed coat from his handkerchief (156), thus confirming the symbol's "nosological", i.e. masculine, implications. Just as the threadbare coat symbolised the hero's emasculation, so the new coat is now unequivocally identified as a symbol of defiant masculinity, denoting the belated escape from under the female "shoe" of the clerk who even at birth had given notice of his future rebellion by "crying and grimacing" at the prospect of life as a Titular Counsellor (142). Hence, we may assume, the unshod state of one of the *khozyayka's* feet when he later returns from the party (162). And we also observe the modesty on this occasion with which she holds her nightshirt to her chest when rushing to the door. Is not this feminine gesture a direct response to his "terrible knocking", to the masculine power that it seems to connote? Is it not thus implied that although the hero by this time has been stripped of his coat, he has been momentarily transformed, like the Kovalyov who recovers his nose, from a victim into a "hunter" of the female? And do we not perceive here evidence of a connection between this scene and the picture that catches his eye earlier as he makes his way to the party? Like the *khozyayka*, we note, the beautiful woman in the picture has also discarded one of her *bashmaki*,[26] while instead of a "small bald patch" her male admirer is endowed with the characteristic hirsuteness (splendid side-whiskers and a "handsome imperial" (159)) of a Gogolian "hunter". Does the picture not symbolise the change that has taken place in the hero and in his attitude to the female, the reversion to normal sexual roles that is briefly reflected in the *khozyayka's* reaction to his knocking?

All these questions, it is suggested, merit affirmative answers, but we can hardly justify them unless we can reconcile them with the spectacle that greets the "landlady's" eyes when she opens the door — the spectacle not of a hirsute admirer, but of the familiar figure of her husband with his sparse hair completely dishevelled. How do we reconcile the implications attributed to his knocking with his coatless, bedraggled appearance? In order to resolve this problem, we must examine the sequence of events that commences with the overcoat's completion.

Predictably the delivery of the completed overcoat evokes a spontaneous female riposte: "Rather sharp frosts were just beginning and were seemingly threatening to be even more severe" (156). This immediate deterioration of the climate plainly harmonises with our interpretation of its symbolic role and may be compared, as a manifestation of the all-embracing nature of female power, to the obstacles that bestrew the path of the desperate Kovalyov. Indeed, from this moment until the hero's death the story may be viewed as a record of the same kind of eerily all-embracing, conspiratorial campaign against the rebel as that which is mounted against the noseless Major. The *raspekan'ya* of the Important Personage, which combine with the climate to inflict the final blow (167), are merely the culminating stage of a sustained assault on the overcoat and its wearer in which the automata of the hierarchy and, as in "The Nose", the emasculated police-force and medical profession are harmoniously dragooned into suppressive and obstructive action. The participation, for example, of the hero's senior colleagues is revealed by yet another *double entendre* — by their superficial demand that he "celebrate the acquisition of his new overcoat" (*vsprysnut' novuyu shinel'*) which is a demand, in reality, that he "sprinkle it with water" (157). And the metaphor is continued at the celebratory party, which takes place, we observe, in a part of the capital in which women are more prominent than usual.[27] On arriving, the hero is confronted at once in the cloakroom with the spectacle of the conspirators' galoshes arranged in rows and with that of a samovar emitting clouds of "steam" (*par*) (159). Once more the image of water is coupled with that of heat to convert the cloakroom into another kitchen of the "St. Petersburg cooks". The overcoat is to be "steamed" or "stewed" into submission, and accordingly it comes as no surprise to find that when the hero departs, the coat is "lying on the floor" (160). Seen in this context, therefore, the comparison of the "terrible wilderness" in which the coat is wrested from him to "a sea" (161) acquires an unsuspected force, suggesting that the brutal scene that follows is merely an extension of the preceding "festivities" and that the faceless thieves are simply new emissaries of the vengeful female oppressor. Taking up their position "almost under his nose", they appropriately cast him, when their task is completed, into the wet snow.

The parallel with the experiences of the noseless Kovalyov becomes increasingly evident after the loss of the coat, providing an additional indication that the coat and the nose are synonymous symbols. Once more the representatives of authority prove consistently uncooperative, and in each case familiar symbols of emasculation, indicative of their subservience to the higher female control, are clearly in evidence. Thus the sentry on duty at the square is portrayed "leaning on his halberd", is charged by the hero with "sleeping" at his post, and insists that he has seen nothing, thus exposing his short-sightedness (161-2). Similarly the superintendent (*chastnyy*), to whom the hero is significantly referred by his "landlady", is also found to be asleep on two separate occasions and later follows the example of the chief-of-police in "The Nose", astutely absenting himself. In this instance an explanation is offered by the "landlady's" announcement that a girl "who was once her cook" had entered the superintendent's service as a nurse (i.e. implicitly as nurse to the superintendent himself, as his personal "cook", performing the same role as the cook who strips the superintendent in "The Nose" of "all his military armour") (162). When contact with the superintendent, therefore, is finally established, it predictably leads nowhere. Receiving the hero's story "in an extremely strange way", he completely ignores "the main point of the affair" (163).

Clearly the "landlady's" commendation of the superintendent to her distraught husband can only be taken to reflect her resolve that the overcoat will not be recovered — a resolve which is perhaps most obviously conveyed by the reference to the hero's suspicion that coat-thieves are active even under the blanket on his bed (168). It is not difficult, therefore, to deduce why she is so anxious to dissuade him from visiting the district constable (*kvartal'nyy*), who would merely contrive, she argues, to "lead him a dance" (162). Since this is precisely his experience at the hands of the superintendent, her actual reason is plainly quite different — fear that with the constable's aid the coat might indeed be recovered and the sexual roles again reversed. The implication, it would seem, is that the constable is either another troublesome rebel or another "young" male who, like the hero's young colleagues, has yet to be completely subdued, and this conclusion appears to be supported a few lines later by the "good advice" of the clerk in the office who similarly enjoins the hero to avoid the constable on the grounds that although he "might find the overcoat in some way, it would nevertheless remain in the possession of the police unless he (Akaky Akakiyevich — J.B.W.) presented legal proof that it belonged to him" (163). In other words, while acknowledging that the coat, if recovered, would still be withheld by the police, the clerk concedes that the constable is quite capable of finding it. Just as the "landlady", therefore, recommends the unhelpful superintendent, the clerk recommends the Important Personage, claiming that "by writing to and communicating with the appropriate person (*s kem sleduyet*) he can push the matter through more successfully" (163).

Given the known identity of this "appropriate person" from whom the Important Personage takes his orders, it is clearly fitting that the hero's meeting with him should be represented as the next stage in his ordeal by heat and water and that he should be overcome in the general's presence by the kind of "terrible sweat" (166) that overcomes Storchenko in his garden, Shpon'ka during his dream and Chichikov during his negotiations with Korobochka. Emerging from the experience "thoroughly baked" (*raspechen*), he is then subjected to the torments of the blizzard and finally succumbs to the "fever" (*goryachka*) which "thanks to the St. Petersburg climate made more rapid progress than could have been expected" (167). His body, therefore, at last surrenders to the remorseless pressure, receiving its final nudge on the way to the grave from one concluding application of heat — the "poultice" (*priparka*)[28] prescribed by the doctor (168), which parallels the treatment recommended to Kovalyov. And with his final word to the victim, who "was constantly in delirium and fever (literally "heat" (*zharu*))", the doctor obliquely discloses his allegiance to the Teutonic sovereign who has dictated his prescription and inspired the entire relentless campaign: ". . . he announced to him that in thirty-six hours he would inevitably be *kaputt*" (168).

At this point in the tale we are confronted again with essentially the same problem of reconciliation that is posed by the apparent contradiction between the hero's submissive appearance and assertive actions on returning from the party. The problem in this case is that of reconciling the surrender of his body with his subsequent self-assertion in the form of the ghost. Certainly at first sight the transition seems rather abrupt and inadequately motivated, but again appearances are highly deceptive, for in reality the transition is clearly foreshadowed by a second evolving process which coincides with that of the hero's physical decline. Although the acquisition of the new overcoat, as indicated, works an immediate transformation in him, it does not impart at once the strength and exuberance of a "Nozdryovian hunter". Hence, perhaps, the retention of one of their *bashmaki* by the "landlady" and the woman in the picture. The mark of emasculation is still inscribed on his thoughts and actions. At the party, for example, he is plagued by the thought that "it was long past the time at which he usually went to bed" (160); he checks the impetus to chase after a woman whose body is "filled with unusual movement" and "set off again very quietly (*ochen' tikho*) as before" (160); and as he makes his way across the square, he closes his eyes (161). Coexisting, however, with this evidence of continuing weakness is the equally striking evidence of gathering strength: his "strength of character", for instance, and resourcefulness when prevailing on the clerks to admit him to the superintendent (163); his "spirit" (*dukh*) and "presence of mind" (*prisutstviye dukha*)[29] which prove so offensive to the Important Personage that he refers to him as a "young man" (167); and the "foul language" and "dreadful words" addressed to "his Excellency" with which he takes his leave of life (168). Paradoxically, therefore, the weakening of his body under the barrage of "heat" is accompanied by the strengthening of his masculine spirit, and it is this latter process which probably determined the choice of the phrase with which Gogol notes his death: *ispustil dukh* ("emitted his spirit") (168). The acquisition of the overcoat, in short, initiates a process which does not cease with its subsequent loss, and it is precisely this difference between body and spirit that explains the apparent contradiction between the "terrible knocking", which induces the "landlady" to affect subservient feminine gestures, and the hero's dishevelled, snow-drenched appearance, which misleads her into thinking that he is still the same submissive vassal. Chizhevsky's view that Akaky Akakiyevich is destroyed by sinful desire[30] is rightly rejected by Driessen on the grounds that "the hero does not lose himself through the overcoat but finds himself",[31] but the crucial point is that neither the loss of the overcoat nor even the hero's death interrupts this process of self-discovery.

The ghost, therefore, presents itself as the hero's resurrected masculine spirit totally liberated from the burden of his emasculated body. Herein lies the explanation of its flamboyantly "masculine" conduct and of the seemingly absurd order issued to the police — that it must be caught "alive or dead" (170). Now the roles of the principal antagonists are completely reversed as the ghost in its turn usurps the role of the Teutonic Empress, inflicting on her most privileged functionaries the fate which in life it suffered itself in the "wilderness". Now it is the ghost which attacks the eyes and wields the weapon of water, "splashing spray" (*zabryzgal*) into the eyes of the three policemen who almost apprehend it (170) and even usurping control of the "St. Petersburg climate" in its attack on the Important Personage (172). And finding at last in the general's coat a garment appropriate to its newly acquired status, it retires contentedly from the scene, leaving its former wearer but a shadow of his former self.

The only major question that remains concerns the identity of the new ghost which rounds on the "feeble" policeman in the final section of the long concluding paragraph (173). The most popular view among critics at the present time seems to be that this second ghost is "the same robber who stole Akaky Akakiyevich's overcoat earlier",[32] but the truth is probably disclosed, as is so often the case in Gogol's works, by a single phrase — by the statement that it was "much taller" (*gorazdo vyshe rostom*) than the ghost of the hero (174), for exactly the same phrase, we note, is used five pages earlier in reference to the hero's replacement in the government office. Repetitions of this kind are not usually coincidental in Gogol's works, and in this case the implication would appear to be that in the course of these five pages a drama parallel to that of the hero has been taking place in the background — the conversion of a young man, who initially "wrote not in the same upright hand, but in a much more slanting and crooked manner" (169), at first into an emasculated automaton and then into another male rebel equipped with an "enormous moustache" and daunting fist (174). The coda would seem to imply that even with the departure from the scene of the satisfied hero, the spirit of male defiance continues to survive, and what could be more appropriate, we may ask, than that Akaky's replacement as vassal should replace him as rebel?

Interpreted in this manner, the conclusion of the tale plainly reinforces the parallel with "The Nose" that has been drawn throughout this analysis. It supports the contention that "The Overcoat" is essentially a new treatment of the same theme in which Gogol merely elevates to the leading role a different symbol of male masculinity. Like the lost and replaced gun in the anecdote recorded by Annenkov, the lost and replaced overcoat of Akaky Akakiyevich, which in the penultimate version of the story, as Driessen has noted,[33] he commissioned Petrovich to make from a pistol and which in the final version is delivered in a handkerchief, directly parallels Kovalyov's lost and reacquired nose, and in both cases the act of reacquisition signifies the triumph of a lonely male rebel against female authority. What distinguishes "The Overcoat", which Victor Erlich has justly described as Gogol's "most closely woven work of short fiction",[34] is the even more subtly allusive manner in which the presence of this authority is evoked. In one respect, as we have seen, it is evoked in exactly the same way as in "The Nose" — by the symbols of emasculation in the portraits of the hero and almost every other male in the story. These symbols immediately imply a female presence. But a more direct perception of this presence is not so easily achieved despite the fact that eight females are referred to in addition to the female pedestrians on the capital's streets — the hero's mother and god-mother, who inflict on him his meaningful name, his "landlady", her cook, the woman in the picture, the wives of Petrovich and the Important Personage, and Karolina Ivanovna. Only after the most searching scrutiny and comparison of the few details which relate to them do we become aware of the crucial connections between their "portraits" and the portrayal of the story's males and come to recognize in the figure of Karolina Ivanovna not only the counterpart of Podtochina in the plot, but also the explanation incarnate of that weird female omnipresence and unity of female purpose which characterises Gogol's portrayal of St. Petersburg no less in "The Overcoat" than in "The Nose". To a very significant degree, as the analysis has shown, our appreciation of the story's thematic coherence is dependent on the decipherment of a single name — a task in which we are aided simply by the phrase "of German extraction". In this sense the contrast between "Shpon'ka" and "The Overcoat" is extremely strik-ing, and it vividly highlights the tendency towards the increasingly allusive representation of female power to which "Old-World Landowners" and "The Nose" have likewise borne witness — a tendency which is one of the most important developments in the evolution of Gogol's art.

As Richard Peace has observed, the "central device" of Gogol is "to pretend that all is 'surface' ", and the failure to detect or acknowledge this element of pretence, as he argues, explains the major deficiencies that recur in the analyses of Gogol's works by the Russian Formalists, particularly the deficiencies of Boris Eykhenbaum's famous essay on "The Overcoat".[35] It is precisely Eykhenbaum's failure to distinguish between "surface" and "sub-text", i.e. between narrator and author, that explains his most frequently quoted comment on the tale: "The centre of gravity is switched from the plot (which is reduced here to a minimum) to the devices of *skaz*, and the most important comic role is assigned to plays on words which are sometimes limited simply to puns and sometimes developed into small anecdotes."[36] If we confine our scrutiny to the "surface", we cannot but accept this view, but it is hoped that this chapter has adequately substantiated the contrary view that far from being reduced to a minimum, the plot embraces the whole work, sustaining the development of a theme that is often most clearly illuminated precisely by those combinations of details which are regarded by Eykhenbaum as little more than comic appendages. In "The Overcoat" we are again confronted with two distinct voices, the coexistence of which is apparent not only in the recurrent lexical *double entendres*, but in virtually every detail. The result once more is an entire story to which the term *double entendre* may legitimately be extended.

FOOTNOTES TO CHAPTER V

1. P. V. Annenkov, *Literaturnyye vospominaniya* (Leningrad, 1928), pp. 61-2.
2. Cf. the narrator's comment on Shpon'ka: "It may not be amiss for me to mention here that in general he was sparing in his use of words. This may have been due to timidity or to the desire to express himself more elegantly" (I, 291).
3. See Driessen, p. 194, and J. Schillinger, "Gogol''s 'The Overcoat' as a Travesty of Hagiography", *The Slavic and East European Journal*, vol. 16, 1972, pp. 36-41.
4. His death is clearly indicated by the past tense of the verb in the mother's statement: "His father was Akaky . . ." (142).
5. The selection of the diminutive root was a later refinement, for Gogol's earlier versions were "Bashmakevich" and "Bashmakov" (521).
6. See the narrator's comparison of him to "a common fly" (143).
7. Richard Peace, "Gogol and Psychological Realism: *Shinel'*", in *Russian and Slavic Literature*, edited by Richard Freeborn *et al.* (Cambridge, Mass., 1976), pp. 77-8.
8. See the remark of a bystander: "A woman has mounted a man! This woman knows how to ride, I dare say!" (I, 129).
9. See the explicit comparison of Khoma to a "saddle-horse" (II, 185).
10. N. Firsov, *Pugachovshchina: opyt sotsiologo-psikhologicheskoy kharakteristiki* (St. Petersburg-Moscow, n.d.), p. 9.
11. Cf. the "little tails" (*khvostiki*) with which Khivrya's jacket is adorned in "The Sorochintsy Fair" (supra, p. 39).
12. Peace, "Gogol and Psychological Realism: *Shinel'*", p. 72.
13. His inability to change verbs from the first person to the third may be regarded as one of the numerous indications of his estrangement from the world outside his "box".
14. The noun is derived from a compound of the verb *pech'* ("to bake").
15. See the vivid portrayal of his mechanical eating habits (145).
16. See *GDS*, pp. 115-6.
17. See, for example, the reference to Nozdryov's "restless energy and liveliness (*boykost'*) of character" (VI, 71). Even the insects on his estate, which prepare the way for his assault on Chichikov by disturbing his slumbers, are "very lively" (*preboykiye*) (VI, 82).
18. Foma Grigor'yevich's solicitous concern for the welfare of his nose has already been noted; it might also be observed that he is equally attentive to the condition of his boots (*sapogi*) (I, 105).

19. While Petrovich has a "squinting eye" (*krivoy glaz*) (148), the headman is described simply as "one-eyed" (*kriv*) (I, 161), and one of Potyomkin's eyes "squints a little" (*nemnogo kriv*) (I, 235).

20. In the second redaction of the story the image of water was implicitly combined with that of heat in the description of the kitchen as "dirtier than the skin of a peasant on his way to the bath-house" (453).

21. In the final version (148) Gogol, following his usual practice of rendering his meaning increasingly elusive with each successive draft (cf. *GDS*, pp. 15, 35), does not make it so explicitly clear that Petrovich contracted his drinking habits in the wake of his marriage.

22. See his unsuccessful attempts to thread his needle (149).

23. See in this connection his exclamation on failing to thread the needle: "It won't go in, the barbarian; you have worn me out (*uyela ty menya*), you rogue" (149). Not only do the terms "barbarian" (*varvarka*) and "rogue" (*shel'ma*) seem somewhat inappropriate if the referent is taken to be the thread, but the verb *uyela* (literally "has eaten away") echoes the verb *yest* (literally "eats") which is used earlier in the same paragraph to convey the "stinging" effect on the eyes of the spirits in which the stairs are soaked. It is possible, therefore, that Petrovich is abusing here not the thread, but rather the "German woman" whose spirits have had the effect on his eyes which creates the problem.

24. Cf. the "pungent vodka" in which Kovalyov is advised to soak his nose.

25. Cf. Petrovich's inability to hold up his head, as well as his drowsy state and the squinting of his eye, after the weekly alcoholic sprees (i.e. immersions in vodka or spirit) which are a metaphor of the "German woman's" attentions (153-4).

26. It may be noted that in an earlier draft of the story there was also a second picture "which apparently served as a continuation of the first" and in which the "beautiful woman", like the "landlady" at the time of the hero's return, was portrayed undressed and in bed (538).

27. See the narrator's statement: "Pedestrians began to pass by more frequently, even ladies began to appear . . ." (158).

28. The noun is related by its root, of course, to the "steam" (*par*) of the samovar at the party.

29. Cf. the earlier statement that he "derived spiritual nourishment" (*pitalsya dukhovno*) from thinking about the new coat (154).

30. D. Chizhevsky, "About Gogol's 'Overcoat' ", in *Gogol from the Twentieth Century*, edited by Robert A. Maguire (Princeton, 1974), pp. 320-1. Chizhevsky's essay was first published (in Russian) in the journal *Sovremennyye zapiski*, vol. 67 (Paris, 1938), pp. 172-95.

31. Driessen, p. 203.

32. Karlinsky, p. 141. Cf. Leon Stilman's Afterword to Nikolai Gogol, *The Diary of a Madman and Other Stories*, translated by Andrew McAndrew (New York, 1960), p. 321; V. Nabokov, *Nikolai Gogol* (London, 1973), pp. 148-9; and Erlich, p. 153. This view has been challenged by Charles C. Bernheimer, who perceives here simply a "nonconclusion" which "denies any notion of factuality and leaves the reader afloat in a fluid world of shifting metamorphoses" ("Cloaking the Self: the Literary Space of Gogol's *Overcoat*", *PMLA*, 1975, No. 1, p. 59).

33. Driessen, p. 207.

34. Erlich, p. 155.

35. Peace, "Gogol and Psychological Realism: *Shinel*'", p. 64.

36. B. M. Eykhenbaum, *"Skvoz' literaturu"*. *Sbornik statey* (Leningrad, 1924), p. 171.

VI

"THE CARRIAGE"

Although we have argued that Pushkin's term "a joke" is an inappropriate description of "The Nose", most readers would probably find it an entirely acceptable description of "The Carriage", which is one of Gogol's shortest tales, and accordingly be astonished to discover that Tolstoy declared it his "best work".[1] Few critics seem to have agreed with him. Written in 1835 and first published the following year in Pushkin's *Sovremennik*, the story is indeed usually praised as a characteristic example of Gogol's "virtuoso narrative craft",[2] but significant depth of meaning is invariably denied it, and if critics are moved to comment on it at all,[3] they normally content themselves with brief summaries of its plot interspersed with illustrations of the comedy and satire. The only major problem posed by the work, it is held, has little to do with the story itself and concerns simply Gogol's reasons for giving it a place in the cycle of "Petersburg tales", to which neither its theme nor its South Russian setting would seem to entitle it. Like "Shpon'ka" in the context of *Evenings*, it is regarded as an "outsider" in the cycle.

In this chapter an attempt will be made to show that the story is a rather more complex work than this traditional attitude to it would suggest. Not only, it is argued, does it form an integral part of the cycle; it is also, as the American critic John G. Garrard has written, "a paradigm of Gogolian fiction in its style, characterisation, narrative strategy and thematic structure".[4] Once more the claim is made that the narrative of events conceals a deeper level of meaning which constitutes the fundamental theme, and in the light of this theme, it is held, the inclusion of the work in the "Petersburg tales" may be seen to be entirely apt.

Perhaps the first feature of the tale that should be noted is the obvious abundance of military imagery, and it soon becomes apparent that it is performing its usual symbolic role. Indeed, its symbolic function casts light at once on the implications of the contrast that lies at the centre of the work — the contrast between the town of B. and the newly arrived cavalry regiment. As the opening sentence of the tale announces, the soldiers bring into the town a vitality, signified by their profession, which is conspicuously lacking in its male inhabitants. It is true that its senior citizen, the mayor (*gorodnichiy*), had once displayed the kind of destructive, "military" aggressiveness of which even Nozdryov would have approved, ordering the trees in every garden to be cut down "to improve the view" (177), but that, we are told, was "in the days of his youth before he had contracted the habit of sleeping immediately after dinner" (178). Now it is his custom, in the narrator's words, to "sleep the whole day through" (179), and our familiarity with Gogol's oblique methods of conveying causes suggests that the first half of the sentence which contains this observation — the reference to the other major representative of local society, the judge, "who lived in the same house with a deacon's wife" — is intended to explain the transformation. The mayor, we may infer, like the judge, has submitted to the authority of a woman and consequently yielded, like Afanasy Ivanovich, Ivan Nikiforovich and the superintendent in "The Nose", to the pleasures of "peace".

It is not only the state of the mayor, however, that seems to be indirectly explained by the judge's domestic situation, for the same propensity to indolence and sleep is ascribed to the male citizenry in general by the symbolic form in which they are clothed — that of "pigs" which, "thrusting their solemn snouts from their baths", fill the streets "at the slightest drop of rain" (177). Yet again we encounter here the image of water, and once more echoes of Chichikov's experience in the domain of Korobochka are immediately striking, providing a pertinent reminder that chapter 3 of *Dead Souls* and "The Carriage" were written at approximately the same time.[5] Again we need to recall the numerous combinations of details in Gogol's works which make it quite plain that neither Chichikov's craving for sleep after being lashed by the symbolic rain and ejected into the sea of mud nor the somnolence of the porcine males of the town of B. is unconnected with their exposure to the element of water, and there can be little doubt that it is precisely in the light of these details that we should regard the apparently gratuitous reference to the habit of the females of the town of gathering in the market-place "with their little scoops" (178). Moreover, since the houses of Gogol's characters are almost invariably symbolic projections of the personalities of their owners, the crumbling of the plaster on the houses in the town "as a result of the rain" (177) may be taken as an additional allusion to the condition of their male occupants.[6] With the aid of the ladies' scoops, the pattern of details suggests, dusty houses are transformed into muddy baths, in which each of the town's males, like Chichikov, is transformed in his turn into a grunting, emasculated pig,[7] into one of "those corpulent animals", as the narrator puts it, "which the local mayor calls Frenchmen" (177) — a term which in Gogol's works, as noted, has distinct connotations of effeminacy. The scene in Korobochka's hen-coop on the morning after Chichikov's arrival directly parallels the situation in the town. There the mud-bespattered Chichikov is metamorphosed into a chick-devouring sow languishing under the surveillance of his female oppressor in the form of a strutting, supercilious cock (VI, 48),[8] and in the description of the town of B., in which the only sign of life is the spectacle of a cock crossing the dusty road (177), the symbols are repeated, alluding once more to an inversion of sexual roles. As in the references to the judge and mayor, the sequence of details seems to imply cause and effect. First the cock crosses the road; then the rain falls, converting the dust into clinging mud; and finally the "pigs" emerge from their domestic "baths" to be plunged, like Chichikov, into the glutinous morass. And they too, it seems, have not only become effeminate but have undergone a change of sex.

The evidence is a symbol of a more overtly sexual character that is inserted into the description of the shops in the square — the image of the *baranki* ("bread rings") which are allegedly to be seen in every shop alongside the invariable female "in a red kerchief" (178)[9] and which remind us of the *bubliki* in the second epigraph of *Mirgorod*.[10] If the meanings that we have ascribed to Praskov'ya Osipovna's "loaves" and the "buns" produced by the "cooks of St. Petersburg" are accepted as valid, we must surely conclude that Gogol would not have introduced this image in such a context, had he not intended it to express a similar meaning. Again the connection with the motif of heat is plainly apparent. At the same time the choice specifically of "bread rings" suggests that the image may equally be related to one of Gogol's less decorous sexual symbols — the obscenity *fetyuk*, derived, according to Gogol's footnote, from the "indecent letter" theta (VI, 76), which Nozdryov hurls at his henpecked brother-in-law Mizhuyev. There is a clear possibility, in other words, that the allusion is to the female genitalia and thus yet again to an inversion of sexual roles, suggesting that the town's males have not only been "baked", but have assumed in the process, like the porcine Chichikov, a distinct female form.

Such, then, is the town into which the regiment brings "colour and life" (178), and in a single sentence, to which the censor took exception, the soldiery's reaction is vividly conveyed: "At the place of execution a soldier with a moustache would probably be soaping the beard of some rural lout, who would merely grunt and look up with popping eyes" (178). Expressing the contempt of the hirsute masculine warriors for the emasculated, grunting urban "pigs", the shaving of their beards may indeed be regarded as a form of execution or, more precisely, as a punishment for their surrender to the "execution" of their masculine personalities. The removal of the hair, we may assume, denotes the removal of the mask which conceals their emasculated condition. But from those males, we observe, who dwell on the fringes of the town the injection of new life elicits a positive, if hesitant, response, not only rousing them from their slumbers but even awakening a renewed passion for such "masculine" activities as gambling which have almost faded from their memories. Thus the narrator announces:

> Neighbouring landowners, whose existence no one hitherto would have suspected, began to visit the town more frequently to see the officers and sometimes to play a game of faro, of which there was only an extremely hazy notion in their heads which were worn out with thoughts of crops, errands for their wives and hares (179).

The implication seems to be that in the society of the officers the landowners are reinitiated in the boisterous habits of their pre-marital, "masculine" youth which, like the mayor, they have been obliged to exchange for "peaceful" anonymity and the privilege of running "errands for their wives".

From the heart of this company of landowners emerges the story's central character equipped with a name that is striking even by Gogolian standards — Pifagor Pifagorovich Chertokutsky. Our initial assumption, of course, is that it was devised for little more than comic effect, that it harmonises with the generally "jocular" character of the tale, but by now it need hardly be repeated that the function of the names of Gogol's characters can rarely be so narrowly defined, and in this case an indication that the name is meaningful is provided before it is even mentioned. Its appearance directly after the portrayal of the town's inhabitants as cocks and pigs suggests the distinct possibility of an allusion to the most famous of Pythagorean tenets — to the philosopher's belief in the transmigration of the soul even from one species to another. The Christian name and patronymic, in short, may plausibly be taken to allude to the symbolic metamorphoses which form a no less prominent and expressive element of the tale than of chapter 3 of *Dead Souls*.

We must obviously suppose, however, that the main significance of the name lies in the information that it imparts about Pifagor Pifagorovich himself. In other words, if our hypothesis is correct, it can only be taken to imply that the hero is himself subject to a metamorphosis, and unambiguous confirmation of the fact is forthcoming from his own lips. Indeed, with his exclamation "Oh, I am a horse!" on waking to find that no arrangements have been made for the dinner to which he invites the officers, he even discloses the form that it takes and thereby highlights his psychological kinship with his urban brethren, for although the latter are portrayed primarily as pigs, they are also attributed with certain equine features by the reference to the walls of their symbolic houses as "skewbald (*pegimi*) instead of white" (177). At the same time, of course, the exclamation also highlights his affinity with Gogol's other heroes who have been "ridden" — above all, with Peter the Great as portrayed in "The Overcoat" — and this affinity is clearly strengthened by the second component of his surname, which is derived from the adjective *kutsyy* ("dock-tailed"). Like Peter, he is not only a "horse", but a "dock-tailed horse".

It comes as no surprise, therefore, to learn that, like Shpon'ka, Afanasy Ivanovich, Ivan Nikiforovich and Manilov, Chertokutsky is a retired officer (179). The combination of details is strikingly familiar and leaves little doubt that the loss of his tail may be related to his retirement, which, like that of his predecessors and Manilov,[11] may be related in its turn to female influence, i.e. to the effects of marriage. As usual in such cases, Gogol withholds explicit information, depending once more on the allusive force of the details and on the sequence in which they are presented, but from the narrator's references to the young Chertokutsky's amorous disposition (179) both the ultimate cause of his "tailless" condition and the identity of the "devil" (*chert*) who inflicted it may be plausibly deduced. And we may also consider in this connection the narrator's seemingly unhelpful comment on the immediate cause of his retirement: "Whether it was he who gave someone a slap in the face in the old days or whether someone gave him a slap, I do not remember for certain: the point is simply that he was asked to retire" (179). The statement seems to imply that his retirement was ordered from above as a punishment for conduct unworthy of an officer, but the symbolism as deciphered thus far provides the basis for a radically different interpretation, suggesting that the allusion may be rather to the marital conflict that preceded the event — to the violence with which his wife insisted on his retirement (the slap that he received), to his initial resistance (the slap that he delivered), and to his eventual submission. Certainly there is again no explicit evidence to support the interpretation, but in the light of the fact that the retired Chertokutsky who presents himself to the reader is now as incapable of administering "slaps" as the retired Manilov, and given Gogol's attested custom of endowing his heroes' wives with "terrible masculine hands", the reading does not seem fanciful. Indeed, it is difficult to think of any other interpretation of the passage that would convincingly explain its inclusion. Foreshadowing the later description by one of the landowners at the general's dinner-party of "a battle such as had never before taken place" (185), the narrator's recollection may be regarded as providing an insight into the kind of sexual conflict from which every male in the town has emerged with his tail effectively docked.

It is true that if we turn to the portrait of the hero's wife, we will again find little obvious support for this interpretation. Although the "half-angry smile" with which she reacts to his late return from the general's dinner-party (185) strikes a slightly sinister note, the overall impression is that of a female who is distinctly feminine and even rather light-headed. It may be recalled, however, that such is also the impression conveyed in "The Nevsky Prospect" by the enticing beauty who has "appropriated the tricks and insolence of a man", and the portraits of Pul'kheriya Ivanovna, Korobochka and Podtochina have already been noted as providing additional confirmation that female masculinity is not always reflected in Gogol's works either in a masculine physique or in overtly masculine conduct. For a more precise indication of the character of Cherto-kutsky's wife we must turn, as usual, to the symbolic motifs which lie at the basis of her portrait, the most revealing of which is contained in the following brief description of her dress and actions when she rises from her bed: ". . . clad in a white dressing-gown, which was draped about her like flowing water, she went into her bathroom, washed in water as fresh as herself and approached her dressing-table" (186). It is inconceivable that the reappearance here of the image of water, in the emphatic form denoted by the duplication, is fortuitous. The association of the image with this "enchanting" female unequivocally relates her to the females of the town with their "little scoops" and thus indirectly explains the term of endearment *pul'pul'tik*, derived from the French *poule* ("hen"), by which she addresses her husband (187). Implicitly identifying her as a "cock", the familiar ornithological symbol plainly lends additional support to our inter-pretation both of the cock in the opening description of the town and of the "contest of slaps" that preceded Chertokutsky's retirement. The allusion once more, we may conclude, is to female victory in the battle for masculine control.

Equally indicative of her relationship with her husband is the dormant condition in which she leaves him. Although the profundity of Chertokutsky's slumbers has an overtly logical explanation in his nocturnal carousing, there are clear indications that Gogol is introducing here the motif of sleep with its usual symbolic meaning. Thus it is noteworthy, for example, that although the hour at which the mistress wakes is not particularly early by rural standards (186), she appears to be the only person on the estate who is not asleep. Even at mid-day the males who are mentioned — the two coachmen and the postilion in addition to her husband — are still snoring resonantly (186), and as she progresses on her walk, displaying, like the cock at the beginning of the tale, the only visible sign of life, it becomes increasingly evident that Gogol is intent here on instilling into this female portrait another of his familiar masculine symbols — the motif of "wakefulness" or "vigilance", which suggests in its turn that the walk is less a stroll than a tour of inspection. Here we see the hero's wife conducting herself in complete conformity with the status that he ascribes to her earlier in his conversation with the general — that of "mistress of the house" (khozyaykoy doma) (184) — as a "mistress" who is concerned less with the beauty of nature than with the security of her domain, with the continuing pacification of her subservient males. Hence her choice of position when she finally sits down — a position "from which there was a clear view of the main road" (186). Like the position of Sobakevich at his spy-window when Chichikov approaches the steps of his house (VI, 94), it implies surveillance, an apprehension of potentially disruptive intruders, and we may accordingly assume that it is precisely this apprehension that explains her "shriek" at the sight of the officers' approaching carriages (187).

Given the symbolic associations of the visitors' profession, this reaction, of course, is entirely appropriate. Like the stentorian response to Chichikov's arrival of the canine sentinels which are an extension of the "mongrel" Koro- bochka's personality, it is the predictable reaction of a masculinized female to the invasion of her realm by emphatically masculine, misogynistic males. But on what intrinsic evidence, it may be asked, can misogyny legitimately be ascribed to these "invaders"? Is the shaving of the town's males the only indicator of their symbolic, misogynistic masculinity? The questions are answered by two remarks of the general — by his rather formal and certainly unenthusiastic response to the prospect of meeting Chertokutsky's wife (184), and by his initial response to the hero's invitation: "I don't know what to say to you in reply. For me to come alone it would be somehow . . . Perhaps you will allow me to come with my fellow officers?" (183). Not only, therefore, is the general evidently a bachelor — a status which in itself is usually indicative in Gogol's works of apprehension of the female — but to the company of females he prefers that of his "masculine" brethren. Hence the absence of females from the dinner-party, which the narrator is careful to note.[12]

Once more, however, the situation turns out to be rather more complex than it seems to be, for it soon becomes apparent that the inference about the general's bachelor status is a little premature. The evidence that prompts this conclusion certainly takes an unusual form, though one that is not entirely unexpected in the context – that of the general's "strong and savage light-grey mare (*gnedaya kobyla*)" (181) which he professes to have owned for two years and which is graced with the unlikely name Agrafena Ivanovna. Considered in relation to the equine element in the portrait of the hero, the clear indication of the horse's sex and the highly formal name suggest that the reader is confronted here with something more than a simple mare, with yet another illustration, in fact, of the Pythagorean tenet. Behind the "savage" equine mask, we may deduce, lies the struggling figure of the general's wife, a direct counterpart of the struggling Chertokutsky who eventually submitted to the slaps of his wife. The two portraits – that of the "dock-tailed" hero and that of the yielding, though still "savage", mare – may be related directly to the contrast that lies at the basis of the story, symbolising respectively the fate of the male in the domain of the masculinized female and that of the female in the military domain of the masculine male. And in the light of this equine symbolism we may perhaps appreciate the force of one of the narrator's earlier observations in the description of the town: "On rare, very rare occasions some landowner . . . clatters over the road in a cross between a britzka and a cart, peeping from behind piled-up bags of flour as he lashes his grey mare (*gneduyu kobylu*) . . ." (177-8). The juxtaposition would suggest that the allusion here is to the beating of wives, which was not only, it seems, a "very rare" sight in the town before the regiment's arrival, but one that was fraught with hazard; hence the perpetrator's need to conceal his identity. No such need, however, is felt by the general. Vehemently criticising the lack of stables in the town in which horses may be groomed and tamed (181), he proudly exposes his "trembling and terrified" mare to public scrutiny.

In his introductory comments on the hero the narrator makes it clear that even the taming of this "dock-tailed" landowner, like that of Agrafena Ivanovna, has yet to be finalised. The masculine instincts of his military youth, it appears, have not yet been completely eradicated. Thus he is still given, we are told, to wearing "a high-waisted dress-coat in the style of a military uniform, spurs on his boots and a moustache under his nose" (179-80), and the nasal sensitivity and hunting instincts of a Nozdryov are apparent in his ability to "smell out (*pronyukhival nosom*) where a cavalry regiment was stationed" (180).[13] But the arrival of the regiment poses the question of how he will react to this more significant restoration of contact with military life. Now, instead of venturing forth in search of regiments, he finds one on his doorstep and even invites its officers to dinner, thereby demonstrating a capacity for masculine self-assertion which his wife had plainly not expected. How will he emerge from this demanding test?

The answer is provided first by his behaviour at the general's dinner-party, and then by his conduct on returning to his estate. The significance of the dinner-party is indicated by parallel episodes in *Dead Souls*, which suggest that it is far more than the convivial occasion that it appears to be. They suggest that it is rather, in fact, a challenge issued by the officers to their civilian guests, an invitation to them to test their powers in the same three quintessentially masculine activities to which the masculine Sobakevich and Nozdryov endeavour to subject the wily Chichikov — eating, drinking and card-playing. In the absence of evidence to the contrary, it must be assumed that the enormous meal, which, apart from the inanimate asparagus and mushrooms, consists entirely of female birds and fish (180), causes Chertokutsky no major problems and that he matches the performance of Chichikov at the house of Sobakevich (VI, 98-100). To the test of the wines, however, which Chichikov succeeds in shirking at the house of Nozdryov with his customary cunning (VI, 75-6), he proves hopelessly unequal, for by the end of the evening it has effectively reduced him to the state of "a man who has no handkerchief in his pocket for his nose" (186). In other words, since the absence of a handkerchief may be taken to imply the absence of a nose (or tail), the ordeal exposes his emasculated condition, his inability to cope with the military or masculine life which is based on gratification of the body's demands. And in the final test which awaits him at the card-table — a test to which Chichikov, despite Nozdryov's abuse, flatly refuses to submit (VI, 81-2) — his weakness seems to be not only confirmed but even explained, for "on two occasions," the narrator reveals, "he threw down a knave instead of a queen" (185). The duplicated action may be viewed as another symbolic exposé of his capitulation in the sexual conflict. While the rejection of the male knave conceivably alludes to the forfeiture of his own masculinity, the retention of the queen, we may conclude, denotes his subservience to the more potent masculinity of the "mistress" (*khozyayka*) of his house. Hence, perhaps, the selection of the knave (*valet*) instead of the king, for if this interpretation is correct, it may be seen to present yet another example of the type of Gogolian *double entendre* which hinges on the tension between the Russian meaning of a word and a different meaning of its non-Russian source. Identifying the former "warrior" as the valet of his masculinized spouse, the term implicitly explains why his head, after he has issued his invitation, is promptly filled with thoughts of "pasties and pies" (183) and why he feels obliged to leave the party at once "in order to prepare everything for the reception of his guests and for the dinner on the morrow" (184). These preoccupations are definitive of his domestic position.

The scene that follows, in which thoughts of pasties vie with the lure of punch and whist, is a dramatization of his psychological conflict, of the struggle within him between the domestic valet and the former officer and knave, and although the punch and whist would seem to prevail, prompting repeated postponements of his departure, their triumph, as we have seen, is belied by his performance. The "low bow" with which he enters his carriage on departing (185) reflects the servility of the valet, while the two burdocks (*repeynika*) that cling to his military moustache seem to symbolise the collapse of his "masculine" aspirations. Meaning not only "burdock" but also the "docked tail" (*kutsyy khvostik*) of a bear, elk or hare,[14] the noun *repeynik* is conceivably inserted here as a culminating allusion to his failure in the "masculine" tests, incidentally explaining, perhaps, why the landowners in general are as much preoccupied with thoughts of hares as with "errands for their wives" (179).

The various allusions, however, to the hero's condition are not yet exhausted, for at this stage in the narrative the most important of his metamophoses has yet to be fully disclosed. It is revealed perhaps most clearly in the scene in which he is roused from his slumbers by his agitated wife. Described at first as sleeping "*mertvetski*" ("like the dead") — an adverb, we may assume, which is as meaningful here as in the brief portrait of Korobochka's coachman in chapter 8 of *Dead Souls* (VI, 177) — he eventually responds to her enquiries about the visitors, we read, with "a slight mooing such as a calf emits when it is trying to find its mother's teats with its snout" and instinctively addresses her as *mon'-munya*. Although this unusual term of endearment is not to be found in the dictionary, it may be plausibly inferred from the context that its source is the Ukrainian noun *monya* which means "milk". The term would seem to reflect, in short, the transformation of the image in the simile into a metaphor. Chertokutsky is not only compared to a calf; he actually becomes one, while his wife is implicitly transformed into his bovine mother, and it is precisely this mother-child relationship which highlights the symbolic meaning of the story's title. Adhering to the practice of conveying the hero's emasculation by means of animal metaphors, Gogol now introduces the additional idea of infantile dependence which he had used with such notable effect in the portrait of Afanasy Ivanovich in "Old-World Landowners", and in the symbol of the *kolyaska*, which means "perambulator" as well as "carriage", we see how the metaphors of horse and child are fused to give birth to a single image.

In the light of this ulterior level of meaning Chertokutsky's earlier conversation about *kolyaski* with the general clearly acquires an importance which is not immediately apparent. His remark in the course of this discussion that to sit in his *kolyaska* is to experience the feeling that "one is being rocked in a cradle by a nurse" (182) is merely the most obvious indication that his thoughts here are centred less on a carriage than on a perambulator. Hence his reference, reminiscent of the reference in "Shpon'ka" to Storchenko's cheeks, to the softness of its *podushki* — a noun meaning "pillows" as well as "cushions" which in the first draft of the tale was significantly linked by means of the verb *potonut'* ("to sink") with the image of water (468). Equally noteworthy is Chertokutsky's description of the manner in which the *kolyaska* came into his possession. He informs the general:

> It was bought by a friend (*drug*) of mine, a rare person (*chelovek*),
> the companion (*tovarishch*) of my childhood with whom you would
> get on perfectly. We are on such terms that our possessions are
> shared mutually. I won it from him at cards (183).

Like the earlier description of the "contest of slaps", the passage can be viewed,
of course, as simply one more example of a typical Gogolian digression. It also
admits, however, of an interpretation which relates it directly to the symbolic
drama that we have perceived in the work. Each of Chertokutsky's remarks here
may be regarded as an illuminating example of the highly deceptive type of
statement that is produced in Gogol's art by the contradictions in his character-
portraits between biological and symbolic sex, by the sexual indeterminacy of
his females who are more masculine than feminine. In respect of the sex of the
referent, of course, the nouns *drug, chelovek* and *tovarishch* are ambiguous
despite their masculine gender, and it seems hardly coincidental that Gogol
should have restricted himself in such a context to three nouns of this particular
type. The following comment on the nature of the relationship conceivably
provides the explanation, for it does not seem unreasonable to suggest that the
phrase "we are on such terms that our possessions are shared mutually" alludes
to the marital contract and thus identifies the referent as the hero's wife, as the
female who in a very real sense is the "companion" of his "childhood", and
neither the suggested affinity of the "friend" with the general nor the reference
to gambling detracts from the plausibility of this conclusion. On the contrary,
they merely confirm the conclusion which has already been reached about her
sexual status, implying equality with the "masculine" officer and a partiality for
his "masculine" activities. According to this interpretation, in other words, the
game of cards is a parallel symbol to the "contest of slaps", a complementary
allusion to the post-marital struggle for masculine supremacy in which the
"prize" was paradoxically awarded to the vanquished contestant. As the winner
of the *kolyaska*, Chertokutsky is exposed as the loser in the game.

The final part of the narrative records the effects of his defeat and of his
failure at the general's dinner-party. On waking the next morning, as we have
seen, he relapses at once into his childlike state, turning first to the breast of his
"mother" and then, on being informed of the officers' imminent arrival, to the
security of his *kolyaska*. He "ran to hide," we read, "in the coach house,
assuming that there his position would be completely secure" and, on alighting,
"covered himself with the apron and leather for greater security and fell
completely silent, curled up in his dressing-gown" (188). Such is the infantile
posture — "curled up in an extraordinary way" (189) — in which the officers
discover him, and it may be noted that the general's surprise is considerably
milder than the spectacle would seem to justify. His request to see the *kolyaska*,
his insistence on inspecting its contents and his brusque, undemonstrative

reaction to the sight that greets his eyes all suggest that he half-expects to find his host in this "unmasculine" position. The motivation, of course, is clearly provided — the hero's performance in the "masculine" tests which have already exposed his emasculated condition. For the general, we may deduce, the visit is little more than a means of confirming his fears.

It need hardly be said, however, that the symbol of the "perambulator" is relevant not only to Chertokutsky. Its obvious connection with the motifs of sleep and "peace" highlights its relevance to the town's entire male populace as described in the opening paragraph, and it may now be understood why the dust-covered road of the town is compared in this paragraph to a "pillow" (*podushka*) (177). The symbol expands, in short, to embrace the whole town, and even in the portraits of the officers the insidious effects on the male of entering this urban "perambulator" are clearly reflected. Not for nothing, one suspects, is the staff-captain at the dinner-party portrayed reclining on a "pillow" (*podushku*) (184), while the last of the carriages which transport the officers to the hero's estate contains "four officers and a fifth in their arms" (186). Even the general, it seems, is not immune, for although he declares himself to be "not particularly well off for carriages (*ekipazhey*)", he confesses to a desire to obtain "a modern *kolyaska*" (182).

The following statement of the general, however, is still more significant, for it enables us to suggest an answer to the question that is most obviously posed by the story: why did Gogol include it in the "Petersburg tales"? The general remarks: "I have written about this matter to my brother who is now in St. Petersburg, though whether he will send one or not I do not know" (182). Having ascertained in our studies of "The Nose" and "The Overcoat" the most salient feature of Gogol's St. Petersburg — the matriarchal structure of its society — we can readily appreciate the major implication of this statement: namely, that the Russian capital is the source of the most effective emasculating *kolyaski*. And in his reply the hero seems to concur with this judgment. Preparing the way for the eulogy of his own *kolyaska*, he comments: "I am of the opinion, your Excellency, that there is no better *kolyaska* than the Viennese (*venskaya*)" (182). Considered in relation to the preceding reference to St. Petersburg, the adjective *venskaya*, like the names "Yakovlevich" and "Ivan" in "The Nose", presents itself as a telling anagram — as an anagram of the epithet *nevskaya* which reinforces the connection of the symbol not only with the capital but also with the image of water. The *kolyaska*, it transpires, in which Chertokutsky is emasculated is related to the symbolic river in which the nose of Kovalyov is unceremoniously dumped.

It is not only, however, through the image of the *kolyaska* that the link with the capital is forged. As we have observed, the other principal metaphor in the hero's portrait — that which is reflected in his surname — is equally significant in this respect, denoting his affinity with the capital's founder as portrayed in the story that immediately precedes "The Carriage" in the "Petersburg tales". It has been argued in the last chapter that the metaphor of the dock-tailed horse, which equates the condition of the Emperor Peter with that of the provincial landowner, alludes to the unprecedented period of female rule in Russia which commenced soon after Peter's death, culminating in the protracted reign of the usurper Catherine. There are grounds for believing that Gogol initially intended to introduce the same allusion into "The Carriage", for in the first draft the hero is described as "one of those landowners whom the owners of small estates approach timidly and almost always with a bow, while those who have large estates and work for Catherine look upon him in a rather sardonic way" (465). Are we not meant to recognize in the two types of landowner respectively the submissive males and supercilious females of the town of B.? Even in the provinces, it seems to be implied, the "workers for Catherine" are busy extending the Empress's female dominion, docking the tails of their males and asserting themselves as queens over subservient valets. Even in the remotest corners of the empire, to repeat the words of the police-captain in the opening paragraph of "The Overcoat", the "institutions of the state are being destroyed". The function of "The Carriage", we may conclude, in the context of the "Petersburg tales" is precisely to confirm the truth of this claim.

FOOTNOTES TO CHAPTER VI

1. L. N. Tolstoy, *Sobraniye sochineniy*, vol. 20 (Moscow, 1965), p. 324.
2. Setchkarev, p. 162.
3. The story is ignored by Erlich and accorded less than a page by Gukovsky.
4. John G. Garrard, "Some Thoughts on Gogol's 'Kolyaska' ", *PMLA*, 1975, No. 5, p. 850.
5. The story was completed, it seems, at the beginning of October 1835, when Gogol sent it to Pushkin. On 7 October he also notified Pushkin that he had suspended work on *Dead Souls* after completing the third chapter (X, 375).
6. Cf. the use of the same symbol in *Dead Souls* to convey the condition of Plyushkin (VI, 112). See *GDS*, p. 114.
7. Cf. the exclamation of the "grandfather" in "A Place Bewitched" (in *Evenings*) when he is soaked in slops by an "infernal woman" (*chertova baba*): "How she has scalded (*oparila*) me! It's as if I were a pig before Christmas" (I, 315).
8. See *GDS*, p. 78.
9. Cf. the "red boots" of the Empress Catherine in "A Lost Letter" (supra, p. 94) and the "red cashmere shawl" that Shpon'ka's aunt is given to wearing "on Easter Sundays and on her name-day" (supra, p. 18).
10. See supra, p. 46.
11. See *GDS*, pp. 62-3.
12. See his remark: "The company consisted of men — officers and certain neighbouring landowners" (179).
13. Cf. the comment on Nozdryov: "His sensitive nose could detect from a distance of several miles where a fair was taking place . . ." (VI, 70).
14. See V. Dal', *Tolkovyy slovar' zhivogo velikorusskogo yazyka*, vol. 4 (Moscow, 1956), p. 92.

CONCLUSION

"Whenever we read anything," writes Northrop Frye, "we find our attention moving in two directions at once." He continues:

> One direction is outward or centrifugal, in which we keep going outside our reading, from the individual words to the things they mean, or in practice to our memory of the conventional associations between them. The other direction is inward, or centripetal, in which we try to develop from the words a sense of the larger verbal pattern they make.

And he concludes: "In all literary structures the final direction of meaning is inward."[1]

These words record the conviction that underlies this study and define its consistent aim: to develop from the words "a sense of the larger verbal pattern they make". In the belief that in literary art, as in all art forms, the creative process involves the activity of "patterning", an attempt has been made to identify the patterns that lie at the basis of the five selected tales. At the same time it need hardly be stated that "pattern by itself does not make literature".[2] Accordingly, it has not been our task to pass judgment on Gogol's art. Our aim has rather been simply to facilitate this task by illuminating the axis on which the seemingly disparate elements of his tales cohere to form an expressive "harmony". In the analyses of all five tales our attention has been directed inward. The answers to the question "why?" have been sought in the fiction itself, and in each case the conclusion has been that a "larger verbal pattern" encompassing the entire narrative can be perceived if the conventional associations between the individual words and "the things they mean" are disregarded. Every creative writer, of course, exploits the tension between the conventional associations of the words he employs and the associations they acquire in the aesthetic context in which he places them, but it is difficult to think of any other writer who exploits this tension as extensively as Gogol and whose art is so dependent on the transformative powers of the aesthetic context. From the most ordinary words, which continually lure the reader's attention outside the text into the world of conventional experience, he constructs within the text a unique metaphorical universe governed by its own aesthetic logic. In the creation of this universe lies Gogol's genius.

The main argument of this study is that the hub of this universe is a vision of evil and human imperfection which receives allegorical expression in the form of a recurrent type of sexual conflict, and the detailed analyses of the five major stories have served to highlight the features of this allegorical art which are considered most important and characteristic. Certainly some sensibilities will be offended by the conclusions. Exception will be taken in particular, one imagines, to the relative neglect in each case of the "surface", i.e. of the conventional associations between words. Yet it would be wrong to infer that the meanings suggested by the "surface" are regarded as unimportant. In combination with the comedy and frequent absurdities, the fractured, digressive character of the facade was plainly designed to evoke a world in which absurdity reigned supreme. The grotesqueness of the facade mirrors the grotesqueness of the world depicted. It has a self-evidently satirical function. But although, as John G. Garrard has observed, "satire and the grotesque are both present and important in Gogol's fiction," neither "allows us to possess all of Gogol or to illuminate the essence of his creation".[3] The assumption that they do, as we have noted, is considered the principal fallacy in the Formalists' studies of Gogol's works, explaining the failure of Zundelovich, Vinogradov and Eykhenbaum respectively to perceive any unifying plot in "Shpon'ka",[4] "The Nose"[5] and "The Overcoat". Restricting his attention to the "surface", to the satire and grotesque, Eykhenbaum has little choice but to contend that words are often combined in "The Overcoat" not on the basis of logical relationships but solely for reasons of sound,[6] and for the same reason we find Setchkarev applying the same judgment forty years later to Gogol's fiction in its entirety.[7] But are we really to believe that Gogol was in the habit of revising his works as many as eight times[8] simply in order to fashion expressive or amusing combinations of sounds? Are we to believe that it was solely considerations of sound that dictated the replacement of "Ivanovich" and "Fyodorovich" with "Yakovlevich" in "The Nose" and "Nastas'ya Karlovna" with "Karolina Ivanovna" in "The Overcoat"? Surely the repeated revisions are more convincingly explained by our definition of the remarkably difficult task that he set himself in each of his major works: that of constructing beneath a mask of digressiveness and absurdity a coherent, logical symbolic drama in which every word and detail is a significant element of meaning. It has been our purpose in this study to determine the nature of this drama, to show that variations of essentially the same drama lie at the basis of his narrative works, and to demonstrate that in each case there is a consistent logic in terms of which the more perplexing aspects of his creative method might be plausibly explained. The result is not an exhaustive study of the meaning of the selected works, but a study of meanings that might be considered primary for the simple reason that they consistently harmonize with the logic of repeated patterns.

Aspiring to remove "some of the layers of critical clichés which all too frequently obscure rather than elucidate Gogol's creations", the American scholar James Bailey has argued the need for a precise methodology in the study of his works. "Each piece," he states, "should first be analyzed as one artistic whole (the work itself), then it should be studied against the background of Gogol's other works (all of Gogol)".[9] It would be difficult to disagree in principle with this method of proceeding, and the interpreter's task would be greatly eased if it could be consistently adopted. But it has been one of the main contentions of this book that in the study of Gogol's works the two stages of the critical exercise that Bailey distinguishes can rarely be separated. The tales of Gogol are not simply far more homogeneous than appearances would suggest; they are essentially the "chapters" of a single composite work with a consistent theme written in an evolving, but basically uniform, symbolic code and, as in *Dead Souls*, the elements of the code do not disclose their meaning in every "chapter". Repeatedly, as we have seen, the task of deciphering them necessitates the collation of details in one "chapter" with the same or similar details in another, and it has emerged from our examination of "Shpon'ka" and the other tales of *Evenings* that without this comparative type of study the early stories are no more comprehensible than the "Petersburg tales". Which story, we may ask, casts the more illuminating light on the other — "Christmas Eve" or "The Overcoat"? One can only reply that neither is fully intelligible without reference to the other. In the same way all Gogol's tales cast light on one another, so that the critic is continually obliged to refer backwards and forwards not only within the individual story, but within the cycle to which it belongs and within the greater whole of which the cycle is a part.

The interpreter's greatest difficulty, therefore, is clearly apparent. Since comparison and collation are his only means of deciphering the code in the almost total absence of explicit disclosures by the author, it follows that the plausibility of his interpretations is largely dependent on the sheer volume of comparative evidence that he succeeds in accumulating. At the same time the comparative evidence that is relevant to the meaning of a given word, detail or combination of details cannot all be adduced at once except at the cost of constant and unacceptably lengthy digressions. By the very nature of the exercise, therefore, substantiation is protracted and cumulative, which means that at least initially the critic is obliged to some degree to crave the reader's indulgence, to request that he suspend his scepticism on the tacit understanding that each succeeding analysis will serve to substantiate further the conclusions that have been reached. Such a request is certainly implicit in some of the earlier parts of this study, which might well provoke the charge of arbitrary reading. Nor is it difficult to imagine the same charge being voiced by the reader who confines himself to just one of the five analyses. It is hoped, however, that taken together and considered in relation to one another, they will produce a rather different reaction and be judged in the end to have achieved their main objective: that of illuminating the essential features of Gogol's symbolic narrative art.

FOOTNOTES TO CONCLUSION

1. Northrop Frye, *Anatomy of Criticism* (Princeton, 1957), pp. 73-4.
2. D. Daiches, *A Study of Literature for Readers and Critics* (London, 1948), p. 80.
3. Garrard, p. 850.
4. See Ya. Zundelovich, "Poetika groteska", in *Problemy poetiki*, edited by V. Ya. Bryusov (Moscow-Leningrad, 1926), p. 76.
5. See V. V. Vinogradov, *Evolyutsiya russkogo naturalizma. Gogol' i Dostoyevsky* (Leningrad, 1929), p. 7.
6. Eykhenbaum, pp. 178, 181.
7. Setchkarev, p. 220.
8. See N. V. Berg, "Vospominaniya o N. V. Gogole", in *Gogol' v vospominaniyakh sovremennikov* (Moscow, 1952), p. 506.
9. James Bailey, "Some Remarks about the Structure of Gogol's 'Overcoat' ", in *Mnemozina. Studia litteraria russica in honorem Vsevolod Setchkarev*, edited by J. T. Baer and N. W. Ingham (Munich, 1974), p. 20.

SELECT BIBLIOGRAPHY

The list given below contains the books and articles on Gogol that are referred to in this study and the works that I have generally found most informative. For a fuller bibliography of critical works on Gogol's short fiction the reader is referred to Driessen, pp. 233-41.

Abramovich, G. L., " 'Starosvetskiye pomeshchiki' N. V. Gogolya", *Uchenyye zapiski Moskovskogo oblastnogo pedagogicheskogo instituta*, vol. 40, 1956, pp. 33-48.
Annenkov, P. V., *Literaturnyye vospominaniya* (Leningrad, 1928).
Bailey, J., "Some Remarks about the Structure of Gogol's 'Overcoat' ", in *Mnemozina. Studia litteraria russica in honorem Vsevolod Setchkarev*, edited by J. T. Baer and N. W. Ingham (Munich, 1974), pp. 13-22.
Belyy, A., *Masterstvo Gogolya* (Moscow, 1934).
Bernheimer, C. C., "Cloaking the Self: the Literary Space of Gogol's *Overcoat*", *PMLA*, 1975, No. 1, pp. 53-61.
Bowman, H. E., "The Nose", *The Slavonic and East European Review*, vol. 31, 1952, pp. 204-11.
Brodiansky, Nina, "Gogol' and His Characters", *The Slavonic and East European Review*, vol. 31, 1952, pp. 36-57.
Chizhevsky, D., "Neizvestnyy Gogol' ", *Novyy zhurnal*, vol. 27, 1952, pp. 126-58.
De Jonge, A., "Gogol' ", in *Nineteenth-Century Russian Literature*, edited by J. Fennell (London, 1973), pp. 69-129.
Driessen, F. C., *Gogol as a Short-Story Writer. A Study of His Technique of Composition* (Paris-The Hague, 1965).
Erlich, V., *Gogol* (New Haven and London, 1969).
Eykhenbaum, B. M., *"Skvoz' literaturu". Sbornik statey* (Leningrad, 1924).
Fanger, D., "The Gogol Problem: Perspectives from Absence", in *Slavic Forum. Essays in Linguistics and Literature*, edited by M. S. Flier (The Hague-Paris, 1974), pp. 103-29.
————, *The Creation of Nikolai Gogol* (Cambridge, Mass., 1979).
Garrard, J. G., "Some Thoughts on Gogol's 'Kolyaska' ", *PMLA*, 1975, No. 5, pp. 848-59.
Gippius, V. V., *Gogol'* (Leningrad, 1924).
Gogol from the Twentieth Century, edited by R. A. Maguire (Princeton, 1974).
Gogol' v vospominaniyakh sovremennikov (Moscow, 1952).
Grigor'yev, A., *Literaturnaya kritika* (Moscow, 1967).
Gukovsky, G. A., *Realizm Gogolya* (Moscow-Leningrad, 1959).
Hippisley, A., "Gogol"s 'The Overcoat': a Further Interpretation", *The Slavic and East European Journal*, vol. 20, 1976, pp. 121-9.
Holquist, J. M., "The Devil in Mufti: the *Märchenwelt* in Gogol's Short Stories", *PMLA*, 1967, No. 4, pp. 352-62.
Hulanicki, L., " 'The Carriage' by N. V. Gogol' ", *Russian Literature*, vol. 12, 1975, pp. 61-77.
Karlinsky, S., *The Sexual Labyrinth of Nikolai Gogol* (Cambridge, Mass., and London, 1976).
Kolb-Seletski, N. M., "Gastronomy, Gogol and His Fiction", *The Slavic Review*, vol. 29, 1970, pp. 34-57.
Mandel'shtam, I., *Kharakter gogolevskogo stilya* (Helsingfors, 1902).

McLean, H., "Gogol's Retreat from Love: Toward an Interpretation of 'Mirgorod' ", in *American Contributions to the Fourth International Congress of Slavists* (The Hague, 1958), pp. 225-44.

Merezhkovsky, D. S., *Gogol' i chert* (Moscow, 1906).

Mills, J. O., "Gogol's 'Overcoat': the Pathetic Passages Reconsidered", *PMLA*, 1974, No. 5, pp. 1106-11.

Mochul'sky, K., *Dukhovnyy put' Gogolya* (Paris, 1934).

Myshkovskaya, L., "Khudozhestvennyye osobennosti satiry Gogolya", in *Masterstvo russkikh klassikov. Sbornik statey* (Moscow, 1959), pp. 62-121.

Nabokov, V., *Nikolay Gogol* (London, 1973).

Nikolay Vasil'yevich Gogol'. Sbornik statey, edited by A. N. Sokolov (Moscow, 1954).

Nilsson, N. A., "Gogol's *The Overcoat* and the Topography of Petersburg", *Scando-Slavica*, vol. 21, 1975, pp. 5-18.

N. V. Gogol' v russkoy kritike (Moscow, 1953).

Oulianoff, N. I., "Arabesque or Apocalypse? On the Fundamental Idea of Gogol's Story *The Nose*", *Canadian Slavic Studies*, vol. 1, 1967, pp. 158-71.

Peace, R., "Gogol's *Old World Landowners*", *The Slavonic and East European Review*, vol. 53, 1975, pp. 504-20.

———, "Gogol and Psychological Realism: *Shinel'* ", in *Russian and Slavic Literature*, edited by Richard Freeborn *et al.* (Cambridge, Mass., 1976), pp. 63-91.

Poggioli, R., "Gogol's 'Old-Fashioned Landowners': an Inverted Eclogue", *Indiana Slavic Studies*, vol. 3, 1963, pp. 54-75.

Rowe, W. W., *Through Gogol's Looking Glass: Reverse Visions, False Focus, and Precarious Logic* (New York, 1976).

Rozanov, V. V., *Legenda o velikom inkvizitore*, 3rd edn. (St. Petersburg, 1906).

Schillinger, J., "Gogol''s 'The Overcoat' as a Travesty of Hagiography", *The Slavic and East European Journal*, vol. 16, 1972, pp. 36-41.

Setchkarev, V., *Gogol. His Life and Works* (London, 1965).

Slonimsky, L., *Tekhnika komicheskogo u Gogolya* (Petrograd, 1923).

Spycher, P. C., "N. V. Gogol's 'The Nose': a Satirical Comic Fantasy Born of an Impotence Complex", *The Slavic and East European Journal*, vol. 7, 1963, pp. 361-74.

Stilman, L., "Gogol's 'Overcoat' – Thematic Pattern and Origins", *American Slavic and East European Review*, vol. 11, 1952, pp. 138-48.

———, "Afterword", in Nikolai Gogol, *The Diary of a Madman and Other Stories*, translated by Andrew McAndrew (New York, 1960).

———, "Nevesty, zhenikhi i svakhi", *Vozdushnyye puti*, vol. 4 (New York, 1965), pp. 198-211.

Tynyanov, Yu., "Dostoyevsky i Gogol'. (K teorii parodii)", in his *Arkhaisty i novatory* (Leningrad, 1929), pp. 412-55.

Veresayev, V., *Kak rabotal Gogol'* (Moscow, 1934).

Vinogradov, V. V., *Gogol' i natural'naya shkola* (Leningrad, 1925).

———, *Evolyutsiya russkogo naturalizma. Gogol' i Dostoyevsky* (Leningrad, 1929).

———, "Yazyk Gogolya", in *N. V. Gogol'. Materialy i issledovaniya*, edited by V. V. Gippius, vol. 2 (Moscow-Leningrad, 1936), pp. 286-376.

———, "O yazyke ranney prozy Gogolya", in *Materialy i issledovaniya po istorii russkogo literaturnogo yazyka*, vol. 2 (Moscow-Leningrad, 1951), pp. 94-138.

Woodward, J. B., *Gogol's "Dead Souls"* (Princeton, 1978).

———, "Allegory and Symbol in Gogol''s Second Idyll", *The Modern Language Review*, vol. 73, 1978, pp. 351-67.

———, "The Symbolic Logic of Gogol''s *The Nose*", *Russian Literature*, vol. 7, 1979, pp. 537-64.

Yeremina, V. I., "N. V. Gogol' ", in *Russkaya literatura i fol'klor (pervaya polovina XIX v.)* (Leningrad, 1976), pp. 249-91.

Yermakov, I. D., *Ocherki po analizu tvorchestva N. V. Gogolya* (Petrograd, 1923).

Zundelovich, Ya., "Poetika groteska", in *Problemy poetiki*, edited by V. Ya. Bryusov (Moscow-Leningrad, 1926), pp. 61-79.